1,000,000 Books
are available to read at

Forgotten Books

www.ForgottenBooks.com

Read online
Download PDF
Purchase in print

ISBN 978-0-243-42443-6
PIBN 10795319

This book is a reproduction of an important historical work. Forgotten Books uses state-of-the-art technology to digitally reconstruct the work, preserving the original format whilst repairing imperfections present in the aged copy. In rare cases, an imperfection in the original, such as a blemish or missing page, may be replicated in our edition. We do, however, repair the vast majority of imperfections successfully; any imperfections that remain are intentionally left to preserve the state of such historical works.

Forgotten Books is a registered trademark of FB &c Ltd.
Copyright © 2018 FB &c Ltd.
FB &c Ltd, Dalton House, 60 Windsor Avenue, London, SW19 2RR.
Company number 08720141. Registered in England and Wales.

For support please visit www.forgottenbooks.com

1 MONTH OF FREE READING

at

www.ForgottenBooks.com

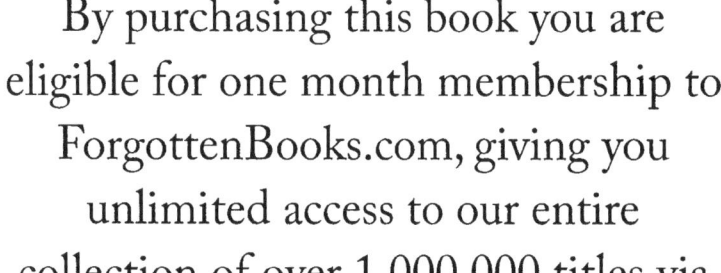

By purchasing this book you are eligible for one month membership to ForgottenBooks.com, giving you unlimited access to our entire collection of over 1,000,000 titles via our web site and mobile apps.

To claim your free month visit:
www.forgottenbooks.com/free795319

* Offer is valid for 45 days from date of purchase. Terms and conditions apply.

English
Français
Deutsche
Italiano
Español
Português

www.forgottenbooks.com

Mythology Photography **Fiction**
Fishing Christianity **Art** Cooking
Essays Buddhism Freemasonry
Medicine **Biology** Music **Ancient Egypt** Evolution Carpentry Physics
Dance Geology **Mathematics** Fitness
Shakespeare **Folklore** Yoga Marketing
Confidence Immortality Biographies
Poetry **Psychology** Witchcraft
Electronics Chemistry History **Law**
Accounting **Philosophy** Anthropology
Alchemy Drama Quantum Mechanics
Atheism Sexual Health **Ancient History**
Entrepreneurship Languages Sport
Paleontology Needlework Islam
Metaphysics Investment Archaeology
Parenting Statistics Criminology
Motivational

LIBRARY OF CONGRESS.

PR 3383

Chap.......... Copyright No..........

Shelf....A3.M3

1893

UNITED STATES OF AMERICA.

Laurel-Crowned Letters.

The Best Letters of Lord Chesterfield.

The Best Letters of Madame de Sévigné.

The Best Letters of Lady Mary Wortley Montagu.

The Best Letters of Horace Walpole.

The Best Letters of Charles Lamb.

The Best Letters of Percy Bysshe Shelley.

The Best Letters of William Cowper.

OTHER VOLUMES IN PREPARATION.

UNIFORM IN STYLE. PRICE, $1.00 PER VOLUME.

THE BEST LETTERS

OF

WILLIAM COWPER

Edited with an Introduction

By ANNA B. McMAHAN

CHICAGO
A. C. McCLURG AND COMPANY
1893

COPYRIGHT
BY A. C. MCCLURG AND CO.
A.D. 1892

CONTENTS.

		PAGE
INTRODUCTION		7

LETTER		
I.	Descriptive of his Situation at Huntingdon	19
II.	On his Illness and Recovery	21
III.	Concerning a Book of Meditations	23
IV.	First Acquaintance with the Unwin Family	24
V.	More about the Unwins	26
VI.	On becoming a Member of the Unwin Family	29
VII.	Manner of Life with the Unwins	30
VIII.	Motives for introducing Unwin to his Grand Kinsfolk	33
IX.	Death of the Rev. Morley Unwin	35
X.	Concerning Gray and his Works	36
XI.	Concerning Unrequited Obligations	37
XII.	A Budget of Home News	38
XIII.	On Mr. Newton's Removal from Olney	40
XIV.	A Night Adventure. — Enclosing New Poem	43
XV.	Explanation of Delay. — Pope's Letters	46
XVI.	Concerning his own State of Mind	48
XVII.	Concerning his First Volume of Poems	51
XVIII.	Concerning the Trials of publishing Poetry	52
XIX.	His own State of Mind compared with Mr. Newton's	58
XX.	Congratulations on the Birth of a Son	61
XXI.	Emotions at the Sight of the Sea	64
XXII.	Dislike of Imitation	66
XXIII.	An Imaginary Conversation	68
XXIV.	England and America	71
XXV.	Dr. Johnson's "Lives of the Poets"	72
XXVI.	Concerning Lady Austen	76

CONTENTS.

LETTER		PAGE
XXVII.	Concerning the Preface to his "Poems." — Lady Austen	79
XXVIII.	Lady Austen. — Sunday Routs	83
XXIX.	The Sweetness of Praise from Friends	86
XXX.	Enclosing a Letter from Benjamin Franklin	89
XXXI.	Ambition for an Olney Reputation	93
XXXII.	Olney Charities. — John Gilpin	95
XXXIII.	A Group of Olney Politicians. — England and America	98
XXXIV.	Restoration of Friendship between Kings of England and France	101
XXXV.	Reflections on the Peace	103
XXXVI.	Doubts concerning the Future Prospects of America	106
XXXVII.	American Loyalists. — Prospects of the United States	108
XXXVIII.	Olney News. — Anticipations of Balloon-travelling	112
XXXIX.	First Introduction to the Throckmortons	116
XL.	A Visit from a Candidate	119
XLI.	Beattie. — Blair. — The Origin of Language	122
XLII.	Enclosing the Manuscript of "The Task"	126
XLIII.	Poem on School Education	128
XLIV.	Concerning a Motto for "Tirocinium"	131
XLV.	On the Death of Mrs. Hill	132
XLVI.	Defending the Title of "The Task" and of its Separate Books	132
XLVII.	John Gilpin. — Vanity of Popular Applause	137
XLVIII.	Rewards of Fame	139
XLIX.	Providential Connection with Mr. Newton	142
L.	Description of his Summer-house	145
LI.	Favorable Reception of his Volume by the Public	146
LII.	Self-Abasement. — "The Task" not advertised	150
LIII.	Reasons for publishing "The Letter to Joseph Hill"	155
LIV.	Revival of an Old Friendship	157
LV.	Concerning Money and Friendship	160
LVI.	Translation of Homer no longer secret	164
LVII.	Happiness in renewing an Old Friendship	165
LVIII.	Reasons for Translating Homer. — Hope of Better Days	170
LIX.	Personal Efforts in behalf of Homer Subscriptions	174

CONTENTS.

LETTER		PAGE
LX.	Review of his Past Life	177
LXI.	Arrangements for his Cousin's Coming to Olney. — Homer. — The Critics	187
LXII.	Lodging Hunting; Part of the Vicarage secured	190
LXIII.	Description of the Vicarage	197
LXIV.	Joy in Lady Hesketh's Letters. — Cowpership .	201
LXV.	Intended Removal to Weston	203
LXVI.	Fuseli. — Homer. — Dennis	207
LXVII.	Unhealthfulness of Olney. — State of his Mind	210
LXVIII.	Concerning Reproof from Mr. Newton . . .	213
LXIX.	Removal from Olney to Weston	216
LXX.	Comforts of the New Abode	219
LXXI.	Death of Rev. William Unwin	221
LXXII.	Illness. — Dreams. — First Acquaintance with Mr. Rose	223
LXXIII.	Thanks for a Copy of Burns	226
LXXIV.	Arrival of a New Vicar at Olney	227
LXXV.	Song on the Slave-Trade. — Hannah More . .	229
LXXVI.	On the Loss of his Library	230
LXXVII.	Thanks for Prints of Crazy Kate and the Lacemaker	231
LXXVIII.	Anticipating a Visit. — Thurlow. — Beau and the Water-Lily	233
LXXIX.	Five Hundred Celebrated Authors	236
LXXX.	Completion of the Iliad, and Beginning of the Odyssey	238
LXXXI.	Occupations previous to becoming Poet . . .	239
LXXXII.	Changes, especially at the Place of his Birth .	242
LXXXIII.	Mrs. Unwin's Accident. — The King's Illness	246
LXXXIV.	Absorption in Homer	248
LXXXV.	Dissatisfaction with his own Writing. — Unconscious Plagiarism	249
LXXXVI.	Stanzas on the Queen's Visit to London presented to Her Majesty	251
LXXXVII.	On the Receipt of a Hamper (in the Manner of Homer)	252
LXXXVIII.	Summary of his Present Situation	254
LXXXIX.	First Appearance of the French Revolution .	256
XC.	Forebodings of the Month of January	257
XCI.	On receiving a Present of his Mother's Picture .	259
XCII.	Acknowledging Receipt of his Mother's Picture	262

LETTER		PAGE
XCIII.	Concerning Two Poems	265
XCIV.	Change of Style in Homer Translation	267
XCV.	Forbidding any Application for the Laureateship	269
XCVI.	Comments on the French Revolution	270
XCVII.	On sending Homer Translation to the Publisher	271
XCVIII.	Epigram on Ill Success of his Subscription at Oxford	273
XCIX.	Success of his Homer. — Correspondence with Thurlow concerning it	274
C.	Engagement to edit Milton	278
CI.	Mrs. Unwin stricken with Paralysis	279
CII.	Lines for an Album. — Departure of the Throckmortons from Weston	280
CIII.	Beginning of Friendship with William Hayley	282
CIV.	Sudden Friendships. — Invitation to Weston	284
CV.	Mrs. Unwin's Second Paralytic Stroke	286
CVI.	Eventfulness of the Last Two Months	287
CVII.	Publisher's Schemes. — Politics	290
CVIII.	Annotations of Homer	293
CIX.	Intrusive Strangers. — Literary Co-operation	295
CX.	Principles of Translation	297
CXI.	Stanzas to Mrs. Unwin	300

INTRODUCTION.

WILLIAM COWPER, as a poet, is far less popular than he was two generations ago. When he died, in the first year of the present century, the world was inclined to exclaim, with Byron, —

"What! must deserted Poesy still weep
Where her last hopes with pious Cowper sleep?"

Biographers arose in numbers; but as each wrote to counteract what he considered the dangerous heresies of the others, little progress was made towards gaining a complete picture of the man. All of them dealt with the same facts; namely, that as a boy Cowper was of a delicate physical constitution and highly sensitive temperament, ill-fitted for the life of the public school to which he was sent when six years old, on the death of his mother; that after leaving school some fifteen years drifted away, ostensibly in the study and practice of the law, but really in idleness and frivolity; that when a relative procured him a government appointment which required a preliminary appearance at the bar of the House of Lords, his strangely nervous nature succumbed at the prospect of such an ordeal, his reason gave way, and it became necessary to commit him wholly to medical care and supervision; that after eighteen months in a private insane asylum his mind had in some degree recovered its balance, and he came forth a changed man, resolved to renounce forever the old London life, and to devote himself to religious pursuits; that the remainder of his days were passed in almost total seclusion from the world; that his old malady, taking the form of suicidal mania, returned at intervals and for longer or shorter periods throughout his life; that until he was fifty years old he had never thought of writing for publication, but that during the ten years that followed he devoted himself to poetical production with such success that he became the most popular poet of his time.

But the interpretations and explanations of these facts were as various as the characters of the men by whom they were offered. First came Hayley, Cowper's intimate friend during his last ten years, who was bent on making a Life which should be consistent, and because melancholy when he knew it, therefore melancholy throughout; then Grimshawe, who, regarding Hayley's picture as not sufficiently pious, rewrote the tale with the addition of much cant and twaddle, in order to meet "the demands and expectations of the religious public;" then Southey, more competent than either, who wrote with a fulness of detail amounting to prolixity, but still, like the others, failed to disclose any connection between the poet's life and the poet's work. Whichever of these early tales we read, the main impression left with us is that of a man of weak yet tenacious character, unsteady mind, and melancholy temperament; a pensive being, born to be a recluse; a half-feminine figure, without acquaintance with men or experience of life; a hypochondriac, sick in body and sick in soul, who yet wrote poems full of sweetness and sanity, — poems which all the world loved to read, which brought him praise and friends and gold, a pension from government, and numbers of admiring disciples eager to sit at his feet.

A generation later, and we encounter a new set of critics and a new phase of criticism. Ideals of poetry have changed; readers of the new time find " The Task " a *task* indeed. Some of them are even so bold as to deny that it is a great poem, and to wonder at the taste of their good fathers and mothers. Then upon closer observation it began to be noted that even if not great *absolutely* and considered by himself, Cowper was yet a very marked figure *relatively*, as judged by his place in the history of poetry. It began to be suspected that Cowper, so far from taking with him to his grave the "last hopes" of poetry, was indeed but heralding its newest and brightest hopes. Recognizing that a new school of poetry had arisen in England, the greatest that had been known there since the days of Elizabeth, it was proclaimed that to Cowper belonged the distinction of being the first to break through the artificial boundaries that had been raised about the art, and to restore it to its natural allegiance to nature and freedom. It became a favorite theme of the critics to exalt Cowper by depreciating Pope; to show what damage had been wrought by Pope until repaired by Cowper. Sainte-Beuve likened Cowper to Rousseau in the service each had rendered in bringing about the reaction against eighteenth-century codes of taste and morality; Matthew Arnold called him "the precursor of Wordsworth." Such is still the favorite point of view. Scarcely any account of William Cowper as poet omits to give some view of the state of English taste and English verse in the latter half of the eighteenth century, and to show the important place occupied by him in the evolution of modern poetry. Whatever value such inquiries may have for the student of poetry, whatever satisfaction he may find in contemplating a " Period," and in being told that it "began with Cowper's Task, culminated under Wordsworth, and ended with Shelley," it is happily entirely uncalled for as an introduction to Cowper's Letters. Here we have to deal with a man who seemingly lived entirely apart from the currents of thought of his time, who was almost wholly undisturbed by the passing questions and answers of the day. In this respect he is a great contrast to most of the famous letter-writers The letters of Horace Walpole are so full of political allusions, so crammed with references to public men and events, that no one can read them understandingly without some knowledge of the history of the times; those of Madame de Sévigné and Lady Montagu derive a large part of their interest from the fact that these ladies had seen much of life and the world, and that they had a wealth of material from which to draw in their own gay and eventful careers. But Cowper was always notably deficient in any enthusiasm for public transactions, was, indeed, of a temper so incurious that even while yet a London youth, he did not think the most splendid spectacle the metropolis could afford, and which it did afford but once in his life, — the coronation of a king, — worth the little trouble it would have cost him to witness it.

Therefore Cowper's Letters, with a few exceptions, furnish but a barren field if one seeks for reports or even opinions of current events. His reflections on the American war are indeed interesting, since illustrations of the foolishness of prophesying are always entertaining; but his predictions that "the loss of America will be the ruin of England" (Letter XXIV.), and that "the Americans will not be equal to the task of establishing an empire," because forsooth "she has no great men" (Letter XXXVII.), can hardly be said to conduce to Cowper's reputation as a judge of character or affairs.

A leading English critic,[1] speaking of Cowper's poetry, has said: "We read him not for his passion or for

[1] T. H. Ward in "English Poets."

his ideas, but for his love of Nature and his faithful rendering of her beauty; for his truth of portraiture, for his humor, for his pathos; for the refined honesty of his style, for the melancholy interest of his life, and for the simplicity and loveliness of his character." Much the same may be said of his letters. Although not written for publication (for he begged his correspondents to burn them, and would have been dismayed at the thought of these confidences of friendship coming to the eye of the world), yet they are as elegant and classic as the most finished compositions. Every one bears the impress of truth; he never exaggerates for the sake of effect. Both his humor and his pathos are spontaneous, and impart a glow to a multitude of trifles in themselves colorless. So frankly and artlessly self-revealing are they, that we come very close indeed to an uneventful but most interesting life, to a character very unusual truly, but far less out of harmony with his writings than the formal biographies would lead us to suppose. When we read the letters, we lose sight of the conventional Cowper,— a poor creature, composite of fanatic, madman, and recluse, melancholy from his birth, and, throughout his life, feeble of purpose, capricious, and obstinate, — but we gain instead a figure much more consistent with the sweetness and vitality of Cowper's poetry.

With one exception, there is scarcely an episode in his career of which we have not some account in the letters, given by the man himself in his confidences to one or another of his friends. This exception is his youthful love for his cousin Theodora Cowper. Certain poems, however, partly supply the deficiency. Many love verses he wrote to her in their happy days ; and when all intercourse was at an end between them, and the lady in deference to the paternal command neither saw nor heard from her lover more, she carefully preserved these precious tokens of his devotion She survived him twenty-four years; but when she too had passed away, some relatives published them in a small volume. They are now to be found in all complete editions of the poems; and the pathetic story may be partly read between the lines of the "Delia" verses, in the poems called "Of Himself" and "On the Death of Sir Wm. Russell," wherein occurs the passage so well known to all readers of poetry:—

> "Still, still I mourn, with each returning day,
> Him snatched by fate in early youth away,
> And her, through tedious years of doubt and pain,
> Fixed in her choice, and faithful, but in vain!"

Cowper was fond of reminiscences in his letters; his memories extend back to a bright but brief period in early childhood when he had still a mother. She died when he was six years old (1737); but the blank that was left in his life, and the filial tenderness with which he cherished her memory are shown when he writes, at the age of fifty, that she has never been out of his thoughts for a week altogether during that long half-century. The child seems to have lived at home very little afterward; and his next four years were very miserable, owing to the persecutions he underwent at the public school, to which he was sent immediately, notwithstanding his tender years. Possibly some of the experiences of that time did permanent injury to a constitution naturally delicate and a disposition naturally timid, and indeed may have had not a little to do with that morbid self-consciousness which afterward developed in such painful forms.

But with the termination of these unhappy experiences, the twenty-two years that followed seem to have been more than commonly free from the sorrows and anxieties that not even youth can escape He went to school at Westminster, at precisely the most brilliant period of its history: he excelled at cricket and football, was liked by everybody, and formed friendships that lasted as long as he lived. Afterward, apprenticed to an attorney, he had for a fellow clerk and jovial companion in the office, Edward Thurlow, a brilliant youth, afterward Lord Chancellor; he spent much time with Theodora and her two sisters at the house of their father and his uncle, Ashley Cowper, a man influential in high places; he became a lawyer on his own account, and though without clients, seems not to have grieved greatly thereat. He belonged to a "Nonsense Club:" he joined with some lively fellows of the old Westminster set in writing chatty articles for a literary periodical of theirs, called "The Connoisseur;" he went to Brighton, to the play, was careless of his money. It is hard to find any signs of melancholy, or any premonitions which serve as an explanation of what followed. Nevertheless, the first of those attacks of madness which beset him through life was close at hand. Mental disease was little understood in those days, and at this distance of time it is extremely difficult to comprehend the situation. Had there been a Maudsley or a Hammond to consult in the case, the first inquiry would probably have been directed towards the family history, and we should know whether the ancestral records included any earlier instances of mental trouble or even eccentricity. As it is, plenty of theories have been offered, but none show a cause in any degree proportioned to the effect. One thing only is plain, that the malady, whatever its origin, finally assumed the form of religious mania. He believed that he was an outcast from God, and that it was the divine will that he should put an end to his own existence. When he failed to accomplish this purpose (the garter breaking with which he tried to hang himself), he considered that his failure was fatal to his reconciliation, and that henceforth he was everlastingly damned. Although this delusion yielded in a few months to judicious medical treatment, yet it was the ever-recurring torment of his after life, the special and horrible hallucination that took possession of him whenever, for any cause, his reason succumbed and his naturally sweet nature became "jangled, out of tune, and harsh."

Such intense and bitter suffering could not well pass without leaving a permanent shadow; but the epithets "gloomy," "pious," "melancholy," "mad," habitually prefixed to Cowper's name, emphasize out of all due proportion the sad side of the situation. That he was much changed from his former merry and thoughtless self is true; but the testimony of familiar letters to private friends is not to be gainsaid. Except those written when the "fever of the brain" was upon him, they indicate for the most part a mind at peace with itself and a heart full of tenderness for others. As a rule, they reveal unmistakably a gentle, lovable nature, a cheerful philosophy, and a sound good sense. They sparkle with playfulness, they have a tone of habitual thankfulness. It is the hard fate of the insane to belie themselves, to wear a terrible disguise over their natural features; and Cowper was no exception to the rule. The loving grateful heart, the clear reason, the hopeful piety, all yielded to the assaults of the insidious fever; and he became under its domineering influence morose, fanciful, desponding, mistrustful alike of God and man.

The story of the years that follow is told by himself in the letters here selected, and told with so much of detail that it is hardly necessary to summarize it here. Some little introduction to his correspondents, however, may be of service to the reader. Letters derive their tone quite as much from the person addressed as from the person writing, and the individuality of the recipient is an important factor in any epistolary composition.

Lady Hesketh, whose name appears oftenest, was one of the three girl cousins, daughters of Ashley Cowper, at whose house Cowper had spent so much time in his London days to the neglect of the law, but to his own great enjoyment. As the sister of Theodora, as well as for her own endearing qualities, there is greater tenderness and intimacy in Cowper's manner to her than to any other. She was already married to Sir Thomas Hesketh before the beginning of their correspondence; afterward it was interrupted for many years, during which she had been absent from England, had become a widow, and been much occupied by mournful duties. It is plain, however, that many years of separation and broken intercourse were without power to lessen the ties that bound these kinsfolk together in youth. She is described as a woman of brilliant beauty, high spirits, and warm heart.

The letters to Joseph Hill extend over a very long series of years. Hill was a friend of Westminster days, a man of solid, practical sense, looking after Cowper's business affairs in London all his life, but also a man of bright wit, one of the seven members of the Nonsense Club. He seems to have well deserved the praise of Cowper's lines in the "Epistle,"—

"An honest man close-buttoned to the chin,
Broadcloth without, and a warm heart within."

Rev. William Cawthorne Unwin was the first of the Unwin family with whom Cowper made acquaintance, as described in Letters IV. and V. In the year following the death of the elder Unwin, and soon after the removal of the family to Olney, the young clergyman took charge of a parish at Stock in Essex; and from that time until his death, twenty years later, a constant correspondence was maintained. Cowper's own feeling is indicated in a letter where he says: "I have had more comfort, far more comfort, in the connections that I have formed within the last twenty years than in the more numerous ones that I had before. Memorandum: The latter are almost all Unwins or Unwinisms." Alexander Knox, speaking of their correspondence, says: "I suppose there are not in the world letters equal in merit, as compositions, to those of Cowper to Unwin."

Rev. John Newton was a curate, for the sake of whose spiritual guidance the Unwin family, of which Cowper had now become a member, took up their residence at Olney. Some of the biographers are rather severe upon this pious and well-meaning preacher, as being the direct agent in bringing on Cowper's second and longest spell of insanity (1773-1782). Benham, whose "Life" prefixed to the Globe edition of the Poems is in many ways so admirable, says: "Calvinistic doctrine and religious excitement threw an already trembling mind off its balance, and aggravated a malady which but for them might probably have been cured." But is not this rather a sweeping statement when there was besides such an unfortunate combination of physical conditions existing? Cowper's letters written during the Olney period of his life show that there could hardly have been a more unfavorable residence for a nervous invalid. The house itself was like a prison; its principal sitting-room was over a cellar often filled with water. The surrounding country was low, damp, and miasmatic. During several months of the year it was impossible to go out of doors. There was no pleasant, neighborly society, except during the brief period that Lady Austen lived there. Putrid fevers abounded among the poorer classes of the inhabitants. All the influences, external and internal, were enervating and depressing, and of a tendency to feed his disease. Mr. Newton was six years Cowper's senior, and in some ways his companionship was a helpful one; whether or not it was wholly desirable, the younger man always regarded it as an occasion for gratitude, and expressed himself to the elder with affection tempered with a certain degree of awe and reverence.

It was at the close of this second illness that Cowper began to cultivate his poetical powers He had indeed written a few occasional verses earlier, but now he was encouraged to more sustained efforts by the affectionate solicitude of friends. It was Mrs. Unwin who proposed the undertaking as well as the first themes. His own feelings while writing and publishing his first volume are sufficiently described in the letters. Lady Austen was the source of his inspiration for his second volume and his longest poem, " The Task " It is characteristic of Cowper that he always needed some spur from without; except in his translation of Homer, he seems never to have determined his own work for himself; but he pursued it with great energy and faithfulness when once undertaken. There is perhaps no more touching circumstance in his life than the persistency with which he drudged away with his pen when he felt the creative impulse dying out in his last sad, weak days, hoping for the restoring influence that poetry-writing had proved to him formerly. He courted the Muse, not in search of fame or money, but in search of health.

This is not the place to add anything to that favorite subject of gossip, the relations of Cowper to Mrs. Unwin and to Lady Austen. Whether he ever wished to marry either or neither, whether there was or was not any jealousy between the two women, whether either ever regarded him with any other feeling than that of a protecting and helpful friendship, it is not profitable to inquire nor important to know The general course of his life shows that he had a great capacity for attracting friends, both men and women. Even after his best days were over, a new circle, mostly young men, gathered about him eager to serve him, although often at great personal sacrifice to themselves. "Dear Mr. Cowper" was the way they habitually spoke of him. The cloud which enveloped him and which sometimes broke with such fury over him was owing not to fault but to misfortune; the undeserved and probably needless sufferings of the man awaken towards him a peculiarly pitiful regard, and lodge him tenderly in our hearts forever, even while we grant that many of his themes have lost their hold and much of his verse has ceased to charm.

A. B. McM.

August, 1892.

THE BEST LETTERS

OF

WILLIAM COWPER.

I.

DESCRIPTIVE OF HIS SITUATION AT HUNTINGDON.

To Joseph Hill, Esq., Cook's Court, Carey Street, London.

HUNTINGDON, *June* 24, 1765.

DEAR JOE, — The only recompense I can make you for your kind attention to my affairs during my illness is to tell you that by the mercy of God I am restored to perfect health both of mind and body. This I believe will give you pleasure; and I would gladly do anything from which you could receive it.

I left St. Alban's[1] on the seventeenth, and arrived that day at Cambridge, spent some time there with my brother, and came hither on the twenty-second. I have a lodging that puts me continually in mind of our summer excursions; we have had many worse, and except the size of it (which however is sufficient

---

[1] Where he had spent eighteen months in a private insane asylum, under the care of Dr. Cotton.

for a single man), but few better.[1] I am not quite alone, having brought a servant with me from St. Alban's, who is the very mirror of fidelity and affection for his master. And whereas the Turkish Spy says he kept no servant because he would not have an enemy in his house, I hired mine because I would have a friend. Men do not usually bestow these encomiums on their lackeys, nor do they usually deserve them; but I have had experience of mine, both in sickness and in health, and never saw his fellow.

The river Ouse (I forget how they spell it) is the most agreeable circumstance in this part of the world; at this town it is, I believe, as wide as the Thames at Windsor; nor does the silver Thames better deserve that epithet, nor has it more flowers upon its banks, these being attributes which in strict truth belong to neither. Fluellin would say they are as like as my fingers to my fingers, and there is salmon in both. It is a noble stream to bathe in, and I shall make that use of it three times a week, having introduced myself to it for the first time this morning.

I beg you will remember me to all my friends, which is a task will cost you no great pains to execute; particularly remember me to those of your own house, and believe me

Your very affectionate.

[1] Huntingdon had been chosen as a place of residence because of its nearness to Cambridge, where his brother, John Cowper, lived, and in order that frequent visits might be exchanged.

II.

ON HIS ILLNESS AND RECOVERY.

To Lady Hesketh.

HUNTINGDON, *July* 1, 1765.

MY DEAR LADY HESKETH, — Since the visit you were so kind as to pay me in the Temple (the only time I ever saw you without pleasure), what have I not suffered! And since it has pleased God to restore me to the use of my reason, what have I not enjoyed! You know by experience, how pleasant it is to feel the first approaches of health after a fever; but, oh, the fever of the brain! To feel the quenching of that fire is indeed a blessing which I think it impossible to receive without the most consummate gratitude. 'Terrible as this chastisement is, I acknowledge in it the hand of an infinite justice; nor is it at all more difficult for me to perceive in it the hand of an infinite mercy likewise: when I consider the effect it has had upon me, I am exceedingly thankful for it, and, without hypocrisy, esteem it the greatest blessing, next to life itself, I ever received from the divine bounty. I pray God that I may ever retain this sense of it; and then I am sure I shall continue to be, as I am at present, really happy.

I write thus to you that you may not think me a forlorn and wretched creature; which you might be apt to do, considering my very distant removal from every friend I have in the world, — a circumstance which, before this event befell me, would undoubtedly have made me so; but my affliction has taught me a road to happiness which without it I should never have found; and I know, and have experience of it every day, that the mercy of God, to him who believes himself the object of it, is more than sufficient to compensate for the loss of every other blessing.

You may now inform all those whom you think really interested in my welfare, that they have no need to be apprehensive on the score of my happiness at present. And you yourself will believe that my happiness is no dream, because I have told you the foundation on which it is built. What I have written would appear like enthusiasm to many, for we are apt to give that name to every warm affection of the mind in others which we have not experienced in ourselves; but to you, who have so much to be thankful for, and a temper inclined to gratitude, it will not appear so.

I beg you will give my love to Sir Thomas,[1] and believe that I am obliged to you both for inquiring after me at St. Alban's.

Yours ever.

[1] The husband of Lady Hesketh.

III.

CONCERNING A BOOK OF MEDITATIONS.

To Lady Hesketh.

HUNTINGDON, *August* 17, 1765.

You told me, my dear cousin, that I need not fear writing too often, and you perceive I take you at your word. At present, however, I shall do little more than thank you for the Meditations, which I admire exceedingly: the author of them manifestly loved the truth with an undissembled affection, had made a great progress in the knowledge of it, and experienced all the happiness that naturally results from that noblest of all attainments. There is one circumstance, which he gives us frequent occasion to observe in him, which I believe will ever be found in the philosophy of every true Christian: I mean the eminent rank which he assigns to faith among the virtues, as the source and parent of them all. There is nothing more infallibly true than this; and doubtless it is with a view to the purifying and sanctifying nature of a true faith, that our Saviour says, "He that believeth in me hath everlasting life," with many other expressions to the same purpose. Considered in this light, no wonder it has the power of salvation ascribed to it! Considered in any other, we must suppose it to operate like an oriental talisman, if it obtains for us the least advantage; which is an affront to him who insists upon our having it, and will on no other terms admit us to his favor. I mention this distinguishing article in his Reflections the rather, because it serves for a solid foundation to the distinction I made, in my last, between the specious professor and the true believer, between him whose faith is his Sunday-suit and him who never puts it off at all, — a distinction I am a little fearful sometimes of making, because it is a heavy stroke upon the practice of more than half the Christians in the world.

My dear cousin, I told you I read the book with great pleasure, which may be accounted for from its own merit; but perhaps it pleased me the more because you had travelled the same road before me. You know there is such a pleasure as this, which would want great explanation to some folks, — being perhaps a mystery to those whose hearts are a mere muscle, and serve only for the purposes of an even circulation.

IV.

FIRST ACQUAINTANCE WITH THE UNWIN FAMILY.

To Lady Hesketh.

HUNTINGDON, *September* 14, 1765

MY DEAR COUSIN, — The longer I live here, the better I like the place, and the people who belong to it. I am upon very good terms with no less than five families, besides two or three odd scrambling fellows like myself. The last acquaintance I made here is with the race of the Unwins, consisting of father and mother, son and daughter, the most comfortable social folks you ever knew. The son is about twenty-one years of age, one of the most unreserved and amiable young men I ever conversed with. He is not yet arrived at that time of life when suspicion recommends itself to us in the form of wisdom, and sets everything but our own dear selves at an immeasurable distance from our esteem and confidence. Consequently he is known almost as soon as seen, and having nothing in his heart that makes it necessary for him to keep it barred and bolted, opens it to the perusal even of a stranger. The father is a clergyman, and the son is designed for orders. The design, however, is quite his own, proceeding merely from his being and having always been sincere in his belief and love of the Gospel. Another acquaintance I have lately made is with a Mr. Nicholson, a North Country divine, very poor, but very good and very happy. He reads prayers here twice a day, all the year round; and travels on foot to serve two churches every Sunday through the year, his journey out and home again being sixteen miles. I supped with him last night. He gave me bread and cheese, and a black jug of ale of his own brewing, and doubtless brewed by his own hands. Another of my acquaintance is Mr. ——, a thin, tall, old man, and as good as he is thin. He drinks nothing but water, and eats no flesh; partly, I believe, from a religious scruple (for he is very religious), and partly in the spirit of a valetudinarian. He is to be met with every morning of his life, at about six o'clock, at a fountain of very fine water, about a mile from the town, which is reckoned extremely like the Bristol spring. Being both early risers, and the only early walkers in the place, we soon became acquainted. His great piety can be equalled by nothing but his great regularity, for he is the most perfect timepiece in the world. I have received a visit likewise from Mr. ——. He is very much a gentleman, well read, and sensible. I am persuaded, in short, that if I had the choice of all England where to fix my abode, I could not have chosen better for myself, and most likely I should not have chosen so well.

. . . .

V.

MORE ABOUT THE UNWINS.

To Lady Hesketh.

HUNTINGDON, *October* 18, 1765.

I WISH you joy, my dear cousin, of being safely arrived in port from the storms of Southampton. For my own part, who am but as a Thames wherry in a world full of tempest and commotion, I know so well the value of the creek I have put into, and the snugness it affords me, that I have a sensible sympathy with you in the pleasure you find in being once more blown to Droxford. I know enough of Miss Morley to send her my compliments; to which, if I had never seen her, her affection for you would sufficiently entitle her. If I neglected to do it sooner, it is only because I am naturally apt to neglect what I ought to do; and if I was as genteel as I am negligent, I should be the most delightful creature in the universe.

I am glad you think so favorably of my Huntingdon acquaintance; they are indeed a nice set of folks, and suit me exactly. I should have been more particular in my account of Miss Unwin, if I had had materials for a minute description. She is about eighteen years of age, rather handsome and genteel. In her mother's company she says little; not because her mother requires it of her, but because she seems glad of that excuse for not talking, being somewhat inclined to bashfulness. There is the most remarkable cordiality between all the parts of the family; and the mother and daughter seem to dote upon each other. The first time I went to the house I was introduced to the daughter alone; and sat with her near half an hour, before her brother came in, who had appointed me to call upon him. Talking is necessary in a *tête-à-tête*, to distinguish the persons of the drama from the chairs they sit on: accordingly she talked a great deal, and extremely well; and, like the rest of the family, behaved with as much ease of address as if we had been old acquaintance. She resembles her mother in her great piety, who is one of the most remarkable instances of it I have ever seen. They are altogether the cheerfulest and most engaging family-piece it is possible to conceive.

Since I wrote the above, I met Mrs. Unwin in the street, and went home with her. She and I walked together near two hours in the garden, and had a conversation which did me more good than I should have received from an audience of the first prince in Europe. That woman is a blessing to me, and I never see her without being the better for her company. I am treated in the family as if I was a near relation, and have been repeatedly invited to call upon them at all times. You know what a shy fellow I am; I cannot prevail with myself to make so much use of this privilege as I am sure they intend I should; but perhaps this awkwardness will wear off hereafter. It was my earnest request before I left St. Alban's that wherever it might please Providence to dispose of me, I might meet with such an acquaintance as I find in Mrs. Unwin. How happy it is to believe, with a steadfast assurance, that our petitions are heard even while we are making them; and how delightful to meet with a proof of it in the effectual and actual grant of them! Surely it is a gracious finishing given to those means, which the Almighty has been pleased to make use of for my conversion. After having been deservedly rendered unfit for any society, to be again qualified for it, and admitted at once into the fellowship of those whom God regards as the excellent of the earth, and whom, in the emphatical language of Scripture, he preserves as the apple of his eye, is a blessing which carries with it the stamp and visible superscription of divine bounty, — a grace unlimited as undeserved; and like its glorious Author, free in its course, and blessed in its operation!

My dear cousin ! health and happiness, and above all, the favor of our great and gracious Lord, attend you ! While we seek it in spirit and in truth, we are infinitely more secure of it than of the next breath we expect to draw. Heaven and earth have their destined periods; ten thousand worlds will vanish at the consummation of all things; but the word of God standeth fast; and they who trust in him shall never be confounded.

My love to all who inquire after me.

VI.

ON BECOMING A MEMBER OF THE UNWIN FAMILY.

To Joseph Hill, Esq.

November 5, 1765

DEAR JOE, — I wrote to you about ten days ago,

> Soliciting a quick return of gold,
> To purchase certain horse that like me well.

Either my letter or your answer to it, I fear, has miscarried. The former I hope, because a miscarriage of the latter might be attended with bad consequences.

I find it impossible to proceed any longer in my present course without danger of bankruptcy. I have therefore entered into an agreement with the Rev. Mr. Unwin, to lodge and board with him. The family are the most agreeable in the world. They live in a special good house and in a very genteel way. They are all exactly what I would wish them to be, and I know I shall be as happy with them as I can be on this side of the sun. I did not dream of this matter till about five days ago; but now the whole is settled. I shall transfer myself thither as soon as I have satisfied all demands upon me here.

Yours ever.

I know nobody so like Mrs. Unwin as my Aunt Madan, — I don't mean in person, for she is a much younger woman, but in character.

VII.

MANNER OF LIFE WITH THE UNWINS.

To Mrs. Cowper, at the Park House, Hartford.

HUNTINGDON, *October* 20, 1766.

MY DEAR COUSIN, — I am very sorry for poor Charles's illness, and hope you will soon have cause to thank God for his complete recovery. We have an epidemical fever in this country likewise, which leaves behind it a continual sighing, almost to suffocation; not that I have seen any instance of it, for, blessed be God! our family have hitherto escaped it, but such was the account I heard of it this morning.

I am obliged to you for the interest you take in my welfare, and for your inquiring so particularly after the manner in which my time passes here. As to amusements, I mean what the world calls such, we have none; the place indeed swarms with them, and cards and dancing are the professed business of almost all the *gentle* inhabitants of Huntingdon. We refuse to take part in them, or to be accessaries to this way of murdering our time, and by so doing have acquired the name of Methodists. Having told you how we *do not* spend our time, I will next say how we do. We breakfast commonly between eight and nine; till eleven, we read either the Scripture, or the sermons of some faithful preacher of those holy mysteries; at eleven we attend divine service, which is performed here twice every day; and from twelve to three we separate and amuse ourselves as we please. During that interval I either read in my own apartment, or walk, or ride, or work in the garden. We seldom sit an hour after dinner, but if the weather permits adjourn to the garden, where with Mrs. Unwin and her son I have generally the pleasure of religious conversation till tea-time. If it rains, or is too windy for walking, we either converse within doors, or sing some hymns of Martin's collection, and by the help of Mrs. Unwin's harpsichord make up a tolerable concert, in which our hearts, I hope, are the best and most musical performers. After tea we sally forth to walk in good earnest. Mrs. Unwin is a good walker, and we have generally travelled about four miles before we see home again. When the days are short, we make this excursion in the former part of the day, between church-time and dinner. At night we read and converse, as before, till supper, and commonly finish the evening either with hymns or a sermon; and last of all the family are called to prayers. I need not tell *you* that such a life as this is consistent with the utmost cheerfulness; accordingly we are all happy, and dwell together in unity as brethren. Mrs. Unwin has almost a maternal affection for me, and I have something very like a filial one for her, and her son and I are brothers. Blessed be the God of our salvation for such companions and for such a life; above all, for a heart to like it.

I have had many anxious thoughts about taking orders, and I believe every new convert is apt to think himself called upon for that purpose; but it has pleased God, by means which there is no need to particularize, to give me full satisfaction as to the propriety of declining it; indeed they who have the least idea of what I have suffered from the dread of public exhibitions, will readily excuse my never attempting them hereafter. In the mean time, if it please the Almighty, I may be an instrument of turning many to the truth in a private way, and I hope that my endeavors in this way have not been entirely unsuccessful. Had I the zeal of Moses, I should want an Aaron to be my spokesman.

Yours ever, my dear cousin.

VIII.

MOTIVES FOR INTRODUCING UNWIN TO HIS GRAND KINSFOLK.

To Mrs. Cowper, at the Park House, Hartford.

HUNTINGDON, *April* 3, 1767.

MY DEAR COUSIN, — You sent my friend Unwin home to us charmed with your kind reception of him, and with everything he saw at the Park. Shall I once more give you a peep into my vile and deceitful heart? What motive do you think lay at the bottom of my conduct when I desired him to call upon you? I did not suspect at first that pride and vainglory had any share in it; but quickly after I had recommended the visit to him, I discovered in that fruitful soil the very root of the matter. You know I am a stranger here; all such are suspected characters, unless they bring their credentials with them. To this moment, I believe, it is matter of speculation in the place, whence I came and to whom I belong.

Though my friend, you may suppose, before I was admitted an inmate here, was satisfied that I was not a mere vagabond, and has since that time received more convincing proofs of my *sponsibility*, yet I could not resist the opportunity of furnishing him with ocular demonstration of it, by introducing him to one of my most splendid connections; that when he hears me called "that fellow Cowper," which has happened heretofore, he may be able, upon unquestionable evidence, to assert my gentlemanhood, and relieve me from the weight of that opprobrious appellation. Oh, pride! pride! it deceives with the subtlety of a serpent, and seems to walk erect, though it crawls upon the earth. How will it twist and twine itself about, to get from under the Cross, which it is the glory of our Christian calling to be able to bear with patience and good will. They who can guess at the heart of a stranger, and you especially, who are of a compassionate temper, will be more ready, perhaps, to excuse me in this instance, than I can be to excuse myself. But in good truth it was abominable pride of heart, indignation, and vanity, and deserves no better name. How should such a creature be admitted into those pure and sinless mansions, where nothing shall enter that defileth, did not the blood of Christ, applied by the hand of faith, take away the guilt of sin, and leave no spot or stain behind it? Oh, what continual need have I of an almighty, all-sufficient Saviour! I am glad you are acquainted so *particularly* with *all* the circumstances of my story, for I know that your secrecy and discretion may be trusted with anything. A thread of mercy ran through all the intricate maze of those afflictive providences, so mysterious to myself at the time, and which must ever remain so to all who will not see what was the great design of them; at the judgment-seat of Christ the whole shall be laid open. How is the rod of iron changed into a sceptre of love!

I thank you for the seeds; I have committed some of each sort to the ground, whence they will soon spring up like so many mementos to remind me of my friends at the Park.

IX.

DEATH OF MR. UNWIN.

Mrs. Cowper, at the Park House, Hartford.

HUNTINGDON, *July* 13, 1767.

MY DEAR COUSIN, — The newspaper has told you the truth. Poor Mr. Unwin, being flung from his horse, as he was going to the church on Sunday morning, received a dreadful fracture on the back part of the skull, under which he languished till Thursday evening, and then died. This awful dispensation has left an impression upon our spirits which will not presently be worn off. He died in a poor cottage, to which he was carried immediately after his fall about a mile from home; and his body could not be brought to his house till the spirit was gone to him who gave it. May it be a lesson to us to watch, since we know not the day nor the hour when our Lord cometh!

The effect of it upon my circumstances will only be a change of the place of my abode. For I shall still, by God's leave, continue with Mrs. Unwin, whose behavior to me has always been that of a mother to a son. We know not yet where we shall settle, but we trust that the Lord, whom we seek, will go before us, and prepare a rest for us. We have employed our friend Haweis, Dr. Conyers of Helmsley in Yorkshire, and Mr. Newton of Olney, to look out a place for us; but at present are entirely ignorant under which of the three we shall settle, or whether under either. I have written to my Aunt Madan, to desire Martin [1] to assist us with his inquiries. It is probable we shall stay here till Michaelmas.

X.

CONCERNING GRAY AND HIS WORKS.

To Joseph Hill, Esq.

April — I fancy the 20*th,* 1777.

MY DEAR FRIEND, — Thanks for a turbot, a lobster, and Captain Brydone : a gentleman who relates his travels so agreeably that he deserves always to travel with an agreeable companion. I have been reading Gray's Works, and think him the only poet since Shakespeare entitled to the character of sublime. Perhaps you will remember that I once had a different opinion of him. I was prejudiced. He did not belong to our Thursday society,[2] and was an Eton man, which lowered him prodigiously in our esteem. I once thought Swift's letters the best that could be

---

[1] Martin Madan, brother of Mrs. Cowper, and chaplain to the Lock Hospital. He was one of the most distinguished of the clergy who, departing from the standard of the church, were adopting that style of preaching which characterized the then rising body of the Methodists.

[2] The Nonsense Club, consisting of seven Westminster men who dined together every Thursday. The set was strictly confined to Westminsters. Gray and Mason, being Etonians, were objects of its literary hostility and butts of its satire.

written; but I like Gray's better. His humor, or his wit, or whatever it is to be called, is never ill-natured or offensive, and yet, I think, equally poignant with the Dean's.

I am yours affectionately.

XI.

CONCERNING UNREQUITED OBLIGATIONS.

To Joseph Hill, Esq.

January 1, 1778.

My dear Friend, — Your last packet was doubly welcome, and Mrs. Hill's kindness gives me peculiar pleasure, not as coming from a stranger to me, for I do not account her so, though I never saw her, but as coming from one so nearly connected with yourself. I shall take care to acknowledge the receipt of her obliging letter, when I return the books. Assure yourself, in the mean time, that I read as if the librarian was at my elbow, continually jogging it, and growling out, Make haste. But as I read aloud, I shall not have finished before the end of the week, and will return them by the diligence next Monday.

I shall be glad if you will let me know whether I am to understand by the sorrow you express, that any part of my former supplies is actually cut off, or whether they are only more tardy in coming in than usual. It is useful even to the rich, to know, as nearly as may be, the exact amount of their income; but how much more so to a man of my small dimensions! If the former should be the case, I shall have less reason to be surprised than I have to wonder at the continuance of them so long.[1] Favors are favors indeed, when laid out upon so barren a soil, where the expense of sowing is never accompanied by the smallest hope of return. What pain there is in gratitude, I have often felt; but the pleasure of requiting an obligation has always been out of my reach.

Affectionately yours.

XII.

A BUDGET OF HOME NEWS

To the Rev. William Unwin, at Stock, Essex.

September 21, 1779.

AMICO MIO, — Be pleased to buy me a glazier's diamond pencil. I have glazed the two frames designed to receive my pine plants; but I cannot mend the kitchen windows, till by the help of that implement I can reduce the glass to its proper dimensions. If I were a plumber I should be a complete glazier; and possibly the happy time may come when I shall be seen trudging away to the neighboring towns with a shelf of glass hanging at my back. If government should impose another tax upon that commodity, I hardly know a business in which a gentleman might

[1] An allusion to the annual allowance made for Cowper's support, by subscription among his relatives, immediately after his removal from St. Alban's

more successfully employ himself. A Chinese, of ten times my fortune, would avail himself of such an opportunity without scruple; and why should not I, who want money as much as any mandarin in China? Rousseau would have been charmed to have seen me so occupied, and would have exclaimed with rapture, "that he had found the Emilius who (he supposed) had subsisted only in his own idea." I would recommend it to you to follow my example. You will presently qualify yourself for the task, and may not only amuse yourself at home, but may even exercise your skill in mending the church windows; which, as it would save money to the parish, would conduce, together with your other ministerial accomplishments, to make you extremely popular in the place.

I have eight pair of tame pigeons. When I first enter the garden in a morning, I find them perched upon the wall, waiting for their breakfast; for I feed them always upon the gravel-walk. If your wish should be accomplished, and you should find yourself furnished with the wings of a dove, I shall undoubtedly find you amongst them. Only be so good, if that should be the case, to announce yourself by some means or other. For I imagine your crop will require something better than tares to fill it.

Your mother and I last week made a trip in a post-chaise to Gayhurst, the seat of Mr. Wright, about four miles off. He understood that I did not much affect strange faces, and sent over his servant on purpose to inform me that he was going into Leicestershire, and that if I chose to see the gardens, I might gratify myself without danger of seeing the proprietor.

I accepted the invitation, and was delighted with all I found there. The situation is happy, the gardens elegantly disposed, the hot-house in the most flourishing state, and the orange-trees the most captivating creatures of the kind I ever saw. A man, in short, had need have the talents of Cox or Langford, the auctioneers, to do the whole scene justice.

Our love attends you all. Yours.

XIII.

ON MR. NEWTON'S REMOVAL FROM OLNEY.

To Mrs. Newton.

March 4, 1780.

DEAR MADAM, — To communicate surprise is almost, perhaps quite, as agreeable as to receive it. This is my present motive for writing to you rather than to Mr. Newton. He would be pleased with hearing from me, but he would not be surprised at it; you see, therefore, I am selfish upon the present occasion, and principally consult my own gratification. Indeed, if I consult yours, I should be silent, for I have no such budget as the minister's, furnished and stuffed with ways and means for every emergency, and shall find it difficult, perhaps, to raise supplies even for a short epistle.

You have observed in common conversation, that the man who coughs and blows his nose the oftenest

(I mean if he has not a cold), does it because he has nothing to say. Even so it is in letter-writing; a long preface, such as mine, is an ugly symptom, and always forebodes great sterility in the following pages.

The vicarage-house became a melancholy object, as soon as Mr. Newton had left it; when you left it, it became more melancholy; now it is actually occupied by another family, even I cannot look at it without being shocked. As I walked in the garden this evening, I saw the smoke issue from the study chimney, and said to myself, that used to be a sign that Mr. Newton was there; but it is so no longer. The walls of the house know nothing of the change that has taken place; the bolt of the chamber-door sounds just as it used to do; and when Mr. Page goes upstairs, for aught I know, or ever shall know, the fall of his foot could hardly, perhaps, be distinguished from that of Mr. Newton. But Mr. Newton's foot will never be heard upon that staircase again. These reflections, and such as these, occurred to me upon the occasion, and though in many respects I have no more sensibility left than there is in brick and mortar, yet I am not permitted to be quite unfeeling upon this subject. If I were in a condition to leave Olney too, I certainly would not stay in it. It is no attachment to the place that binds me here, but an unfitness for every other. I lived in it once, but now I am buried in it, and have no business with the world on the outside of my sepulchre; my appearance would startle them, and theirs would be shocking to me.

Such are my thoughts about the matter. Others are more deeply affected, and by more weighty considerations, having been many years the objects of a ministry which they had reason to account themselves happy in the possession of; they fear they shall find themselves great sufferers by the alteration that has taken place; they would have had reason to fear it in any case. But Mr. Newton's successor does not bring with him the happiest presages, so that in the present state of things they have double reason for their fears. Though I can never be the better for Mr. Page, Mr. Page shall never be the worse for me. If his conduct shall even justify the worst apprehensions that have been formed of his character, it is no personal concern of mine. But this I can venture to say, that if he is not spotless, his spots will be seen, and the plainer, because he comes after Mr. Newton.

We were concerned at your account of Robert, and have little doubt but he will shuffle himself out of his place. Where he will find another, is a question not to be resolved by those who recommend him to this. I wrote him a long letter, a day or two after the receipt of yours, but I am afraid it was only clapping a blister upon the crown of a wig-block.

My respects attend Mr. Newton and yourself, accompanied with much affection for you both.

Yours, dear Madam.

XIV.

NIGHT ADVENTURE OF A GINGERBREAD BAKER. — ENCLOSING A NEW POEM.

To Mrs. Newton.

June, 1780.

DEAR MADAM, — When I write to Mr. Newton, he answers me by letter; when I write to you, you answer me in fish. I return you many thanks for the mackerel and lobster. They assured me in terms as intelligible as pen and ink could have spoken, that you still remember Orchard-side; and though they never spoke in their lives, and it was still less to be expected from them that they should speak, being dead, they gave us an assurance of your affection that corresponds exactly with that which Mr. Newton expresses towards us in all his letters. For my own part, I never in my life began a letter more at a venture than the present. It is possible that I may finish it, but perhaps more than probable that I shall not. I have had several indifferent nights, and the wind is easterly, — two circumstances so unfavorable to me in all my occupations, but especially that of writing, that it was with the greatest difficulty I could even bring myself to attempt it.

You have never yet perhaps been made acquainted with the unfortunate Tom Freeman's misadventure. He and his wife returning from Hanslip fair, were coming down Weston Lane ; to wit, themselves, their horse, and their great wooden panniers, at ten o'clock at night. The horse, having a lively imagination and very weak nerves, fancied he either saw or heard something, but has never been able to say what. A sudden fright will impart activity and a momentary vigor even to lameness itself. Accordingly, he started, and sprung from the middle of the road to the side of it, with such surprising alacrity that he dismounted the gingerbread baker and his gingerbread wife in a moment. Not contented with this effort, nor thinking himself yet out of danger, he proceeded as fast as he could to a full gallop, rushed against the gate at the bottom of the lane, and opened it for himself, without perceiving that there was any gate there. Still he galloped, and with a velocity and momentum continually increasing, till he arrived in Olney. I had been in bed about ten minutes, when I heard the most uncommon and unaccountable noise that can be imagined. It was, in fact, occasioned by the clattering of tin pattypans and a Dutch-oven against the sides of the panniers. Much gingerbread was picked up in the street, and Mr. Lucy's windows were broken all to pieces. Had this been all, it would have been a comedy; but we learned the next morning, that the poor woman's collar-bone was broken, and she has hardly been able to resume her occupation since.

What is added on the other side, if I could have persuaded myself to write sooner, would have reached you sooner; 't is about ten days old.

THE DOVES.

Reasoning at every step he treads,
  Man yet mistakes his way,
While meaner things, whom instinct leads,
  Are rarely known to stray.

One silent eve I wander'd late
  And heard the voice of love;
The turtle thus address'd her mate,
  And soothed the listening dove:

Our mutual bond of faith and truth
  No time shall disengage;
Those blessings of our early youth
  Shall cheer our latest age:

While innocence without disguise,
  And constancy sincere,
Shall fill the circles of those eyes,
  And mine can read them there;

Those ills that wait on all below,
  Shall ne'er be felt by me,
Or gently felt, and only so,
  As being shared with thee.

When lightnings flash among the trees,
  Or kites are hovering near,
I fear lest thee alone they seize,
  And know no other fear.

'T is then I feel myself a wife,
  And press thy wedded side,
Resolved a union formed for life
  Death never shall divide.

But oh! if, fickle or unchaste
  (Forgive a transient thought),
Thou couldst become unkind at last,
  And scorn thy present lot,

No need of lightnings from on high,
   Or kites with cruel beak;
Denied the endearments of thine eye,
   This widow'd heart would break.

Thus sang the sweet sequester'd bird
   Soft as the passing wind;
And I recorded what I heard,
   A lesson for mankind.

The male Dove was smoking a pipe, and the female Dove was sewing, while she delivered herself as above. This little circumstance may lead you, perhaps, to guess what pair I had in my eye.[1]

    Yours, dear Madam.

XV.

EXPLANATION OF HIS DELAY IN WRITING. — POPE'S LETTERS.

To the Rev. William Unwin.

June 8, 1780.

MY DEAR FRIEND, — It is possible I might have indulged myself in the pleasure of writing to you without waiting for a letter from you, but for a reason which you will not easily guess. Your mother communicated to me the satisfaction you expressed in my correspondence, that you thought me entertaining and clever, and so forth. Now, you must know, I love praise dearly, especially from the judi-

---

[1] Rev. William Bull and his wife, friends of the Newtons, whose acquaintance Cowper had recently made.

cious, and those who have so much delicacy themselves as not to offend mine in giving it. But then, I found this consequence attending, or likely to attend, the eulogium you bestowed: if my friend thought me witty before, he shall think me ten times more witty hereafter; where I joked once, I will joke five times, and for one sensible remark I will send him a dozen. Now, this foolish vanity would have spoiled me quite, and would have made me as disgusting a letter-writer as Pope, who seems to have thought that unless a sentence was well turned, and every period pointed with some conceit, it was not worth the carriage. Accordingly he is to me, except in very few instances, the most disagreeable maker of epistles that ever I met with. I was willing, therefore, to wait till the impression your commendation had made upon the foolish part of me was worn off, that I might scribble away as usual, and write my uppermost thoughts, and those only.

You are better skilled in ecclesiastical law than I am. Mrs. Powley desires me to inform her whether a parson can be obliged to take an apprentice; for some of her husband's opposers at Dewsbury threaten to clap one upon him. Now I think it would be rather hard, if clergymen, who are not allowed to exercise any handicraft whatever, should be subject to such an imposition. If Mr. Powley was a cordwainer or a breeches-maker all the week, and a preacher only on Sundays, it would seem reasonable enough, in that case, that he should take an apprentice, if he chose it; but even then, in my poor judgment, he ought to be left to his option. If they mean by an apprentice a pupil whom they will oblige him to hew into a parson, and after chipping away the block that hides the minister within, to qualify him to stand erect in a pulpit, that indeed is another consideration. But still, we live in a free country, and I cannot bring myself even to suspect that an English divine can possibly be liable to such compulsion. Ask your uncle, however; for he is wiser in these things than either of us.

. . . .

Your mother sends her love to all, and mine comes jogging along by the side of it.

XVI.

CONCERNING HIS OWN STATE OF MIND AND INCAPACITY FOR SUSTAINED THINKING.

To the Rev. John Newton.

July 12, 1780.

MY DEAR FRIEND, — Such nights as I frequently spend are but a miserable prelude to the succeeding day, and indispose me, above all things, to the business of writing. Yet with a pen in my hand, if I am able to write at all, I find myself gradually relieved; and as I am glad of any employment that may serve to engage my attention, so especially I am pleased with an opportunity of conversing with you, though it be but upon paper. This occupation, above all others, assists me in that self-deception to which I am indebted for all the little comfort I enjoy; things seem to be as they were, and I almost forget that they never can be so again.

We are both obliged to you for a sight of Mr. ——'s letter. The friendly and obliging manner of it will much enhance the difficulty of answering it. I think I can see plainly that though he does not hope for your applause, he would gladly escape your censure. He seems to approach you smoothly and softly, and to take you gently by the hand, as if he bespoke your lenity, and entreated you at least to spare him. You have such skill in the management of your pen that I doubt not you will be able to send him a balmy reproof that shall give him no reason to complain of a broken head. How delusive is the wildest speculation when pursued with eagerness, and nourished with such arguments as the perverted ingenuity of such a mind as his can easily furnish! Judgment falls asleep upon the bench, while Imagination, like a smug, pert counsellor, stands chattering at the bar, and with a deal of fine-spun, enchanting sophistry, carries all before him.

If I had strength of mind, I have not strength of body for the task which, you say, some would impose upon me. I cannot bear much thinking. The meshes of that fine network, the brain, are composed of such mere spinners' threads in me, that when a long thought finds its way into them, it buzzes, and twangs, and bustles about at such a rate as seems to threaten the whole contexture. No; I must needs refer it again to you.

My enigma will probably find you out, and you

will find out my enigma at some future time. I am not in a humor to transcribe it now. Indeed I wonder that a sportive thought should ever knock at the door of my intellects, and still more that it should gain admittance. It is as if harlequin should intrude himself into the gloomy chamber where a corpse is deposited in state. His antic gesticulations would be unseasonable at any rate, but more especially so if they should distort the features of the mournful attendants into laughter. But the mind long wearied with the sameness of a dull, dreary prospect will gladly fix its eyes on anything that may make a little variety in its contemplations, though it were but a kitten playing with her tail.

You would believe, though I did not say it at the end of every letter, that we remember you and Mrs. Newton with the same affection as ever ; but I would not therefore excuse myself from writing what it gives you pleasure to read. I have often wished indeed, when writing to an ordinary correspondent, for the revival of the Roman custom, — *salutem* at top, and *vale* at bottom. But as the French have taught all Europe to enter a room and to leave it with a most ceremonious bow, so they have taught us to begin and conclude our letters in the same manner. However I can say to you,
   Sans cérémonie,
    Adieu, *mon ami!*

XVII.

CONCERNING HIS FIRST VOLUME OF POEMS.

To the Rev. William Unwin.

May 1, 1781.

. . . .

IN the press, and speedily will be published, in one volume octavo, price three shillings, Poems, by William Cowper, of the Inner Temple, Esq. You may suppose, by the size of the publication, that the greatest part of them have been long kept secret, because you yourself have never seen them; but the truth is, that they are most of them, except what you have in your possession, the produce of the last winter. Two thirds of the compilation will be occupied by four pieces, the first of which sprung up in the month of December, and the last of them in the month of March. They contain, I suppose, in all, about two thousand and five hundred lines; are known, or to be known in due time, by the names of "Table Talk," "The Progress of Error," "Truth," "Expostulation." Mr. Newton writes a Preface, and Johnson is the publisher. The principal, I may say the only reason why I never mentioned to you, till now, an affair which I am just going to make known to all the world (if *that* Mr. All-the-world should think it worth his knowing), has been this, — that till within these few days I had not the honor to know it myself. This may seem strange, but it is true;

for not knowing where to find underwriters who would choose to insure them, and not finding it convenient to a purse like mine to run any hazard, even upon the credit of my own ingenuity, I was very much in doubt, for some weeks, whether any bookseller would be willing to subject himself to an ambiguity that might prove very expensive in case of a bad market. But Johnson[1] has heroically set all peradventures at defiance, and takes the whole charge upon himself. So out I come. I shall be glad of my Translations from Vincent Bourne,[2] in your next frank. My Muse will lay herself at your feet immediately on her first public appearance.

Yours, my dear friend.

XVIII.

CONCERNING THE TRIALS OF PUBLISHING POETRY — PROFLIGACY OF THE CLERGY.

To the Rev. William Unwin.

May 23, 1781.

MY DEAR FRIEND, — If a writer's friends have need of patience, how much more the writer! Your desire to see my Muse in public, and mine to gratify you, must both suffer the mortification of delay. I ex-

---

[1] Joseph Johnson, publisher, St. Paul's Churchyard.
[2] Cowper's teacher of Latin at Westminster. Years afterwards Cowper described him as "the neatest of all men in his versification, though the most slovenly in his person."

pected that my trumpeter would have informed the world by this time of all that is needful for them to know upon such an occasion; and that an advertising blast, blown through every newspaper, would have said, "The poet is coming!" But man, especially man that writes verse, is born to disappointments, as surely as printers and booksellers are born to be the most dilatory and tedious of all creatures. The plain English of this magnificent preamble is, that the season of publication is just elapsed, that the town is going into the country every day, and that my book cannot appear till they return, that is to say, not till next winter.

This misfortune, however, comes not without its attendant advantage: I shall now have, what I should not otherwise have had, an opportunity to correct the press myself; no small advantage upon any occasion, but especially important where poetry is concerned! A single erratum may knock out the brains of a whole passage, and that, perhaps, which of all others the unfortunate poet is the most proud of. Add to this, that now and then there is to be found in a printing-house a presumptuous intermeddler, who will fancy himself a poet too, and what is still worse, a better than he that employs him. The consequence is, that with cobbling, and tinkering, and patching on here and there a shred of his own, he makes such a difference between the original and the copy, that an author cannot know his own work again. Now, as I choose to be responsible for nobody's dulness but my own, I am a little comforted, when I reflect that it will be in my power to prevent all such impertinence; and yet not without your assistance. It will be quite necessary that the correspondence between me and Johnson should be carried on without the expense of postage, because proof sheets would make double or treble letters, which expense, as in every instance it must occur twice, — first when the packet is sent, and again when it is returned, — would be rather inconvenient to me, who, as you perceive, am forced to live by my wits, and to him, who hopes to get a little matter no doubt by the same means. Half-a-dozen franks therefore to me, and *totidem* to him, will be singularly acceptable, if you can, without feeling it in any respect a trouble, procure them for me.

My neckcloths being all worn out, I intend to wear stocks, but not unless they are more fashionable than the former. In that case I shall be obliged to you if you will buy me a handsome stock-buckle, for a very little money; for twenty or twenty-five shillings perhaps a second-hand affair may be purchased that will make a figure at Olney.

I am much obliged to you for your offer to support me in a translation of Bourne. It is but seldom, however, and never except for my amusement, that I translate, because I find it disagreeable to work by another man's pattern; I should at least be sure to find it so in a business of any length. Again, *that* is epigrammatic and witty in Latin which would be perfectly insipid in English; and a translator of Bourne would frequently find himself obliged to supply what is called the turn, which is in fact the most difficult and the most expensive part of the whole composition, and could not perhaps, in many instances, be done with any tolerable success. If a Latin poem is neat, elegant, and musical, it is enough; but English readers are not so easily satisfied. To quote myself, you will find, in comparing the Jackdaw with the original, that I was obliged to sharpen a point which, though smart enough in the Latin, would, in English, have appeared as plain and as blunt as the tag of a lace. I love the memory of Vinny Bourne. I think him a better Latin poet than Tibullus, Propertius, Ausonius, or any of the writers in *his* way, except Ovid, and not at all inferior to *him*. I love him too with a love of partiality, because he was usher of the fifth form at Westminster, when I passed through it. He was so good-natured and so indolent that I lost more than I got by him; for he made me as idle as himself. He was such a sloven, as if he had trusted to his genius as a cloak for everything that could disgust you in his person; and indeed in his writings he has almost made amends for all. His humor is entirely original; he can speak of a magpie or a cat in terms so exquisitely appropriated to the character he draws, that one would suppose him animated by the spirit of the creature he describes. And with all this drollery there is a mixture of rational and even religious reflection at times; and always an air of pleasantry, good-nature, and humanity, that makes him, in my mind, one of the most amiable writers in the world. It is not common to meet with an author who can make you smile, and yet at nobody's expense; who is always entertaining, and yet always harmless; and who, though always elegant, and classical to a degree not always found even in the classics themselves, charms more by the simplicity and playfulness of his ideas than by the neatness and purity of his verse; yet such was poor Vinny. I remember seeing the Duke of Richmond set fire to his greasy locks, and box his ears to put it out again.

I am delighted with your project, but not with the view I have of its success. If the world would form its opinion of the clerical character at large from yours in particular, I have no doubt but the event would be as prosperous as you could wish. But I suppose there is not a member of either house who does not see within the circle of his own acquaintance a minister, perhaps many ministers, whose integrity would contribute but little to the effect of such a bill. Here are seven or eight in the neighborhood of Olney, who have shaken hands with sobriety, and who would rather suppress the church, were it not for the emoluments annexed, than discourage the sale of strong beer in a single instance. Were I myself in Parliament, I am not sure that I could favor your scheme; are there not to be found within five miles of almost every neighborhood parsons who would purchase well-accustomed public-houses, because they could secure them a license, and patronize them when they had done? I think no penalty would prevent the abuse, on account of the difficulty of proof, and that no ingenuity could guard against all the possible abuses. To sum up all in few words, — the generality of the clergy, especially within these last twenty or thirty years, have worn their surcingles so loose, that I verily believe no measure that proposed an accession of privilege to an order which the laity retain but little respect for, would meet with the countenance of the legislature. You will do me the justice to suppose that I do not say these things to gratify a splenetic humor or a censorious turn of mind; far from it, — it may add, perhaps, to the severity of the foregoing observations to assert, but if it does, I cannot help asserting, that I verily believe them to be founded upon fact, and that I am sure, partly from my own knowledge, and partly from the report of those whose veracity I can depend upon, that in this part of the world at least, many of the most profligate characters are the very men to whom the morals, and even the souls of others are entrusted; and I cannot suppose that the diocese of Lincoln, or this part of it in particular, is more unfortunate in that respect than the rest of the kingdom.

Since I began to write long poems, I seem to turn up my nose at the idea of a short one. I have lately entered upon one which, if ever finished, cannot easily be comprised in much less than a thousand lines! But this must make part of a second publication, and be accompanied, in due time, by others not yet thought of; for it seems (which I did not know till the bookseller had occasion to tell me so) that single pieces stand no chance, and that nothing less than a volume will go down. You yourself afford me a proof of the certainty of this intelligence, by sending me franks which nothing less than a volume can fill. I have accordingly sent you one, but am obliged to add, that had the wind been in any other point of the compass, or, blowing as it does from the east, had it been less boisterous, you must have been contented with a much shorter letter, but the abridgment of every other occupation is very favorable to that of writing.

I am glad I did not expect to hear from you by this post, for the boy has lost the bag in which your letter must have been enclosed, — another reason for my prolixity!

Yours affectionately.

XIX.

HIS OWN STATE OF MIND COMPARED WITH MR NEWTON'S. — A NEW SCENE OPENING. — RHYMES FOR MRS. NEWTON

To the Rev John Newton.

August 21, 1781.

MY DEAR FRIEND, — You wish you could employ your time to better purpose, yet are never idle. In all that you say or do, — whether you are alone, or pay visits, or receive them; whether you think, or write, or walk, or sit still, — the state of your mind is such as discovers, even to yourself, in spite of all its wanderings, that there is a principle at bottom whose determined tendency is towards the best things. I do not at all doubt the truth of what you say, when you complain of that crowd of trifling thoughts that pesters you without ceasing; but then you always have a serious thought standing at the door of your imagination, like a justice of peace with the riot-act in his hand, ready to read it, and disperse the mob. Here lies the difference between you and me. My thoughts are clad in a sober livery, for the most part as grave as that of a bishop's servants. They turn too upon spiritual subjects; but the tallest fellow and the loudest among them all is he who is continually crying with a loud voice, *Actum est de te; periisti!* You wish for more attention, I for less. Dissipation itself would be welcome to me, so it were not a vicious one; but however earnestly invited, is coy, and keeps at a distance. Yet with all this distressing gloom upon my mind, I experience, as you do, the slipperiness of the present hour, and the rapidity with which time escapes me. Everything around us, and everything that befalls us, constitutes a variety which, whether agreeable or otherwise, has still a thievish propensity, and steals from us days, months, and years, with such unparalleled address, that even while we say they are here, they are gone. From infancy to manhood is rather a tedious period, chiefly, I suppose, because at that time we act under the control of others, and are not suffered to have a will of our own. But thence downward into the vale of years is such a declivity that we have just an opportunity to reflect upon the steepness of it, and then find ourselves at the bottom.

Here is a new scene opening, which, whether it perform what it promises or not, will add fresh plumes to the wings of time, — at least while it continues to be a subject of contemplation. If the project take effect, a thousand varieties will attend the change it will make in our situation at Olney. If not, it will serve, however, to speculate and converse upon, and steal away many hours, by engaging our attention, before it be entirely dropped. Lady Austen, very desirous of retirement, especially of a retirement near her sister, an admirer of Mr. Scott as a preacher, and of your two humble servants now in the greenhouse, as the most agreeable creatures in the world, is at present determined to settle here. That part of our great building which is at present occupied by Dick Coleman, his wife, child, and a thousand rats, is the corner of the world she chooses, above all others, as the place of her future residence. Next spring twelvemonth she begins to repair and beautify, and the following winter (by which time the lease of her house in town will determine) she intends to take possession. I am highly pleased with the plan, on Mrs. Unwin's account, who, since Mrs. Newton's departure, is destitute of all female connection, and has not, in any emergency, a woman to speak to. Mrs. Scott is indeed in the neighborhood, and an excellent person, but always engaged by a close attention to her family, and no more than ourselves a lover of visiting. But these things are all at present in the clouds. Two years must intervene; and in two years not only this project, but all the projects in Europe may be disconcerted.

>Cocoa-nut naught,
> Fish too dear,
> None must be bought
> For us that are here.

No lobster on earth,
 That ever I saw,
To me would be worth
 Sixpence a claw.

So, dear madam, wait
 Till fish can be got
At a reas'nable rate,
 Whether lobster or not;

Till the French and the Dutch
 Have quitted the seas,
And then send as much
 And as oft as you please.

Yours, my dear Sir.

XX.

CONGRATULATIONS ON THE BIRTH OF A SON. — POEM ON "RETIREMENT" IN HAND. — LADY AUSTEN

To the Rev. William Unwin.

August 25, 1781.

MY DEAR FRIEND, — We rejoice with you sincerely in the birth of another son, and in the prospect you have of Mrs. Unwin's recovery; may your three children, and the next three, when they shall make their appearance, prove so many blessings to their parents, and make you wish that you had twice the number. But what made you expect daily that you should hear from me? Letter for letter is the law of all correspondence whatsoever, and because I wrote last, I have indulged myself for some time in expectation of a sheet from you. Not that I govern myself entirely by the punctilio of reciprocation, but having been pretty much occupied of late, I was not sorry to find myself at liberty to exercise my discretion, and furnished with a good excuse if I chose to be silent.

I expected, as you remember, to have been published last spring, and was disappointed. The delay has afforded me an opportunity to increase the quantity of my publication by about a third; and if my Muse has not forsaken me, which I rather suspect to be the case, may possibly yet add to it. I have a subject in hand, which promises me a great abundance of poetical matter, by which, for want of a something I am not able to describe, I cannot at present proceed with. The name of it is "Retirement;" and my purpose, to recommend the proper improvement of it, to set forth the requisites for that end, and to enlarge upon the happiness of that state of life, when managed as it ought to be. In the course of my journey through this ample theme, I should wish to touch upon the characters, the deficiencies, and the mistakes of thousands who enter on a scene of retirement unqualified for it in every respect, and with such designs as have no tendency to promote either their own happiness or that of others. But as I have told you before, there are times when I am no more a poet than I am a mathematician; and when such a time occurs, I always think it better to give up the point than to labor it in vain. I shall yet again be obliged to trouble you for franks; the addition of three thousand lines, or near that number, having occasioned a demand which I did not always foresee ; but your obliging friend and your obliging self having allowed me the liberty of application, I make it without apology.

The solitude, or rather the duality, of our condition at Olney seems drawing to a conclusion. You have not forgot, perhaps, that the building we inhabit consists of two mansions. And because you have only seen the inside of that part of it which is in our occupation, I therefore inform you that the other end of it is by far the most superb, as well as the most commodious. Lady Austen has seen it, has set her heart upon it, is going to fit it up and furnish it, and if she can get rid of the remaining two years of the lease of her London house, will probably enter upon it in a twelvemonth. You will be pleased with this intelligence, because I have already told you that she is a woman perfectly well bred, sensible, and in every respect agreeable ; and above all, because she loves your mother dearly. It has in my eyes (and I doubt not it will have the same in yours) strong marks of providential interposition. A female friend, and one who bids fair to prove herself worthy of the appellation, comes, recommended by a variety of considerations, to such a place as Olney. Since Mr. Newton went, and till this lady came, there was not in the kingdom a retirement more absolutely such than ours. We did not want company ; but when it came, we found it agreeable. A person that has seen much of the world and understands it well, has high spirits, a lively fancy, and great readiness of conversation, introduces a sprightliness into such a scene as this which, if it was peaceful before, is not the worse for being a little enlivened. In case of illness too, to which all are liable, it was rather a gloomy prospect, if we allowed ourselves to advert to it, that there was hardly a woman in the place from whom it would have been reasonable to have expected either comfort or assistance. The present curate's wife is a valuable person, but has a family of her own, and though a neighbor, is not a very near one. But if this plan is effected we shall be in a manner one family, and I suppose never pass a day without some intercourse with each other.

Your mother sends her warm affections, and welcomes into the world the new-born William.

Yours, my dear friend.

XXI.

EMOTIONS AROUSED BY THE SIGHT OF THE OCEAN — LADY AUSTEN'S INTENDED VISIT TO LONDON.

To the Rev. William Unwin.

September 26, 1781.

MY DEAR FRIEND, — I may, I suppose, congratulate you on your safe arrival at Brighthelmstone; and am the better pleased with your design to close the summer there, because I am acquainted with the place, and, by the assistance of fancy, can without much difficulty join myself to the party, and partake with you in your amusements and excursions.

It happened, singularly enough, that just before I received your last, in which you apprise me of your intended journey, I had been writing upon the subject, having found occasion towards the close of my last poem, called "Retirement," to take some notice of the modern passion for sea-side entertainments, and to direct to the means by which they might be made useful as well as agreeable. I think with you, that the most magnificent object under heaven is the great deep; and cannot but feel an unpolite species of astonishment, when I consider the multitudes that view it without emotion and even without reflection. In all its various forms it is an object of all others the most suited to affect us with lasting impressions of the awful Power that created and controls it. I am the less inclined to think this negligence excusable, because, at a time of life when I gave as little attention to religious subjects as almost any man, I yet remember that the waves would preach to me, and that in the midst of dissipation I had an ear to hear them. One of Shakspeare's characters says, "I am never merry when I hear sweet music." The same effect that harmony seems to have had upon him, I have experienced from the sight and sound of the ocean, which have often composed my thoughts into a melancholy not unpleasing nor without its use. So much for *Signor Nettuno*.

Lady Austen goes to London this day se'nnight. We have told her that you shall visit her; which is an enterprise you may engage in with the more alacrity, because as she loves everything that has any connection with your mother, she is sure to feel a sufficient partiality for her son. Add to this, that your own personal recommendations are by no means small, or such as a woman of her fine taste and discernment can possibly overlook. She has many features in her character which you will admire; but one. in particular, on account of the rarity of it, will engage your attention and esteem. She has a degree of gratitude in her composition, so quick a sense of obligation, as is hardly to be found in any rank of life, and, if report say true, is scarce indeed in the superior. Discover but a wish to please her, and she never forgets it; not only thanks you, but the tears will start into her eyes at the recollection of the smallest service. With these fine feelings she has the most, and the most harmless vivacity you can imagine. In short, she is — what you will find her to be, upon half an hour's conversation with her; and when I hear you have a journey to town in contemplation, I will send you her address.

Your mother is well, and joins with me in wishing that you may spend your time agreeably upon the coast of Sussex.

XXII.

DISLIKE OF IMITATION.

To the Rev. William Unwin.

November 24, 1781.

MY DEAR FRIEND, — ... A French author I was reading last night says, He that has written, will write again. If the critics do not set their foot upon this first egg that I have laid, and crush it, I shall probably verify his observation; and when I feel my spirits rise, and that I am armed with industry sufficient for the purpose, undertake the production of another volume. At present, however, I do not feel myself so disposed; and, indeed, he that would write should read, not that he may retail the observations of other men, but that, being thus refreshed and replenished, he may find himself in a condition to make and to produce his own. I reckon it among my principal advantages, as a composer of verses, that I have not read an English poet these thirteen years, and but one these twenty years. Imitation, even of the best models, is my aversion; it is servile and mechanical, a trick that has enabled many to usurp the name of author who could not have written at all if they had not written upon the pattern of somebody indeed original. But when the ear and the taste have been much accustomed to the manner of others, it is almost impossible to avoid it; and we imitate in spite of ourselves, just in proportion as we admire. But enough of this.

Your mother, who is as well as the season of the year will permit, desires me to add her love. The salmon you sent us arrived safe, and was remarkably fresh. What a comfort it is to have a friend who knows that we love salmon, and who cannot pass by a fishmonger's shop, without finding his desire to send us some a temptation too strong to be resisted!

Yours, my dear friend.

XXIII.

AN IMAGINARY CONVERSATION, — PREDICTION OF THE RUIN OF ENGLAND IN CONSEQUENCE OF THE LOSS OF AMERICA.

To Joseph Hill, Esq.

December 9, 1781.

My dear Friend, — Having returned you many thanks for the fine cod and oysters you favored me with, though it is now morning I will suppose it afternoon, that you and I dined together, are comfortably situated by a good fire, and just entering on a sociable conversation. You speak first, because I am a man of few words.

Well, Cowper, what do you think of this American war?

I. To say the truth, I am not very fond of thinking about it; when I do I think of it unpleasantly enough. I think it bids fair to be the ruin of the country.

You. That's very unpleasant indeed! If that should be the consequence, it will be the fault of those who might put a stop to it if they would.

I. But do you really think that practicable?

You. Why not? If people leave off fighting, peace follows of course. I wish they would withdraw the forces and put an end to the squabble.

Now I am going to make a long speech.

I. You know the complexion of my sentiments upon some subjects well enough, and that I do not look upon public events either as fortuitous, or absolutely derivable either from the wisdom or folly of man. These indeed operate as second causes; but we must look for the cause of the decline or the prosperity of an empire elsewhere. I have long since done complaining of men and measures, having learned to consider them merely as the instruments of a higher Power, by which he either bestows wealth, peace, and dignity upon a nation when he favors it; or by which he strips it of all those honors, when public enormities long persisted in provoke him to inflict a public punishment. The counsels of great men become as foolish and preposterous when he is pleased to make them so, as those of the frantic creatures in Bedlam, when they lay their distracted heads together to consider of the state of the nation. But I go still farther. The wisdom, or the want of wisdom, that we observe or think we observe in those that rule us, entirely out of the question, I cannot look upon the circumstances of this country without being persuaded that I discern in them an entanglement and perplexity that I have never met with in the history of any other, which I think preternatural (if I may use the word on such a subject), prodigious in its kind, and such as human sagacity can never remedy. I have a good opinion of the understanding and integrity of some in power, yet I see plainly that they are unequal to the task. I think as favorably of some that are not in power, yet I am sure they have never yet in any of their speeches recommended the plan that would effect the salutary purpose. If we pursue the war, it is because we are desperate; it is plunging and sinking year after year into still greater depths of calamity. If we relinquish it, the remedy is equally desperate, and would prove I believe in the end no remedy at all. Either way we are undone. Perseverance will only enfeeble us more; we cannot recover the colonies by arms. If we discontinue the attempt, in that case we fling away voluntarily what in the other we strive ineffectually to regain; and whether we adopt the one measure or the other, are equally undone: for I consider the loss of America as the ruin of England. Were we less encumbered than we are at home, we could but ill afford it; but being crushed as we are under an enormous debt that the public credit can at no rate carry much longer, the consequence is sure. Thus it appears to me that we are squeezed to death between the two sides of that sort of alternative which is commonly called a cleft stick, the most threatening and portentous condition in which the interests of any country can possibly be found.

I think I have done pretty well for a man of few words, and have contrived to have all the talk to myself. I thank you for not interrupting me.

     Yours, my dear friend.

XXIV.

POEM ON "FRIENDSHIP" LAID ASIDE.— ENGLAND AND AMERICA.

To the Rev. John Newton.

The last day of 1781.

My dear Friend, —. . . . I shall not bumble Johnson for finding fault with " Friendship," though I have a better opinion of it myself; but a poet is, of all men, the most unfit to be judge in his own cause. Partial to all his productions, he is always most partial to the youngest. But as there is a sufficient quantity without it, let that sleep too. If I should live to write again, I may possibly take up that subject a second time, and clothe it in a different dress. It abounds with excellent matter, and much more than I could find room for in two or three pages.

I consider England and America as once one country. They were so, in respect of interest, intercourse, and affinity. A great earthquake has made a partition, and now the Atlantic Ocean flows between them. He that can drain that ocean, and shove the two shores together, so as to make them aptly coincide, and meet each other in every part, can unite them again. But this is a work for Omnipotence, and nothing less than Omnipotence can heal the breach between us. This dispensation is evidently a scourge to England; but is it a blessing to America? Time may prove it one; but at present it does not seem to wear an aspect favorable to their privileges, either civil or religious. I cannot doubt the truth of Dr. W.'s assertion; but the French, who pay but little regard to treaties that clash with their convenience, without a treaty, and even in direct contradiction to verbal engagements, can easily pretend a claim to a country which they have both bled and paid for; and if the validity of that claim be disputed, behold an army ready landed, and well-appointed, and in possession of some of the most fruitful provinces, prepared to prove it. A scourge is a scourge at one end only. A bundle of thunderbolts, such as you have seen in the talons of Jupiter's eagle, is at both ends equally tremendous, and can inflict a judgment upon the West, at the same moment that it seems to intend only the chastisement of the East.

. . . .

XXV.

CONCERNING DR. JOHNSON'S "LIVES OF THE POETS." — ADVICE TO A FATHER.

To the Rev. William Unwin.

January 17, 1782.

MY DEAR WILLIAM, — I am glad we agree in our opinion of King Critic,[1] and the writers on whom he has bestowed his animadversions. It is a matter of indifference to me whether I think with the world at large or not, but I wish my friends to be of my

[1] Dr. Johnson.

mind. The same work will wear a different appearance in the eyes of the same man, according to the different views with which he reads it; if merely for his amusement, his candor being in less danger of a twist from interest or prejudice, he is pleased with what is really pleasing, and is not over-curious to discover a blemish, because the exercise of a minute exactness is not consistent with his purpose. But if he once becomes a critic by trade, the case is altered. He must then at any rate establish, if he can, an opinion in every mind of his uncommon discernment and his exquisite taste. This great end he can never accomplish by thinking in the track that has been beaten under the hoof of public judgment. He must endeavor to convince the world that their favorite authors have more faults than they are aware of, and such as they have never suspected. Having marked out a writer universally esteemed, whom he finds it for that very reason convenient to depreciate and traduce, he will overlook some of his beauties, he will faintly praise others, and in such a manner as to make thousands, more modest, though quite as judicious as himself, question whether they are beauties at all. Can there be a stronger illustration of all that I have said, than the severity of Johnson's remarks upon Prior, I might have said the injustice? His reputation as an author who, with much labor indeed, but with admirable success, has embellished all his poems with the most charming ease, stood unshaken till Johnson thrust his head against it. And how does he attack him in this his principal fort? I can recollect his very words, but I am much mistaken indeed if my memory fails me with respect to the purport of them. "His words," he says, "appear to be forced into their proper places; there indeed we find them, but find likewise that their arrangement has been the effect of constraint, and that without violence they would certainly have stood in a different order." By your leave, most learned Doctor, this is the most disingenuous remark I ever met with, and would have come with a better grace from Curl or Dennis. Every man conversant with verse-writing knows, and knows by painful experience, that the familiar style is of all styles the most difficult to succeed in. To make verse speak the language of prose, without being prosaic, — to marshal the words of it in such an order as they might naturally take in falling from the lips of an extemporary speaker, yet without meanness, harmoniously, elegantly, and without seeming to displace a syllable for the sake of the rhyme, is one of the most arduous tasks a poet can undertake. He that could accomplish this task was Prior; many have imitated his excellence in this particular, but the best copies have fallen far short of the original. And now to tell us, after we and our fathers have admired him for it so long, that he is an easy writer indeed, but that his ease has an air of stiffness in it, in short, that his ease is not ease, but only something like it, what is it but a self-contradiction, an observation that grants what it is just going to deny, and denies what it has just granted, in the same sentence and in the same breath? But I have filled the greatest part of my sheet with a very uninteresting subject. I will only say that as a nation we are not much indebted, in point of poetical credit, to this too sagacious and unmerciful judge; and that for myself in particular, I have reason to rejoice that he entered upon and exhausted the labors of his office before my poor volume could possibly become an object of them. By the way, you cannot have a book at the time you mention; I have lived a fortnight or more in expectation of the last sheet, which is not yet arrived.

You have already furnished John's memory with by far the greatest part of what a parent would wish to store it with. If all that is merely trivial and all that has an immoral tendency were expunged from our English poets, how would they shrink, and how would some of them completely vanish! I believe there are some of Dryden's Fables which he would find very entertaining; they are for the most part fine compositions, and not above his apprehension; but Dryden has written few things that are not blotted here and there with an unchaste allusion, so that you must pick his way for him, lest he should tread in the dirt. You did not mention Milton's Allegro and Penseroso, which I remember being so charmed with when I was a boy that I was never weary of them. There are even passages in the paradisiacal part of the Paradise Lost, which he might study with advantage. And to teach him, as you can, to deliver some of the fine orations made in the Pandæmonium, and those between Satan, Ithuriel, and Zephon, with emphasis, dignity, and propriety, might be of great use to him hereafter. The sooner the ear is formed, and the organs of speech are accustomed to the various inflections of the voice, which the rehearsal of those passages demands, the better. I should think, too, that Thomson's Seasons might afford him some useful lessons. At least they would have a tendency to give his mind an observing and a philosophical turn. I do not forget that he is but a child. But I remember that he is a child favored with talents superior to his years. We were much pleased with his remarks on your almsgiving, and doubt not but it will be verified with respect to the two guineas you sent us, which have made four Christian people happy. Ships I have none, nor have touched a pencil these three years; if ever I take it up again, which I rather suspect I shall not (the employment requiring stronger eyes than mine), it shall be at John's service.

Yours, my dear friend.

XXVI.

CONCERNING LADY AUSTEN.

To the Rev. William Unwin.

February 9, 1782.

My dear Friend, — ... I have a piece of secret history to communicate which I would have imparted sooner, but that I thought it possible there might be no occasion to mention it at all. When persons for whom I have felt a friendship disappoint and mortify me by their conduct, or act unjustly towards me, though I no longer esteem them friends,

I still feel that tenderness for their character that I would conceal the blemish if I could. But in making known the following anecdote to you, I run no risk of a publication, assured that when I have once enjoined you secrecy, you will observe it.

My letters have already apprised you of that close and intimate connection that took place between the lady you visited in Queen Ann Street and us. Nothing could be more promising, though sudden in the commencement. She treated us with as much unreservedness of communication as if we had been born in the same house and educated together. At her departure she herself proposed a correspondence, and because writing does not agree with your mother, proposed a correspondence with me. This sort of intercourse had not been long maintained, before I discovered, by some slight intimations of it, that she had conceived displeasure at somewhat I had written, though I cannot now recollect it. Conscious of none but the most upright, inoffensive intentions, I yet apologized for the passage in question, and the flaw was healed again. Our correspondence after this proceeded smoothly for a considerable time, but at length having had repeated occasion to observe that she expressed a sort of romantic idea of our merits, and built such expectations of felicity upon our friendship as we were sure that nothing human could possibly answer, I wrote to remind her that we were mortal, to recommend it to her not to think more highly of us than the subject would warrant, and intimating that when we embellish a creature with colors taken from our own fancy, and, so adorned, admire and praise it beyond its real merits, we make it an idol, and have nothing to expect in the end, but that it will deceive our hopes, and that we shall derive nothing from it but a painful conviction of our error. Your mother heard me read the letter, she read it herself, and honored it with her warm approbation. But it gave mortal offence; it received indeed an answer, but such an one as I could by no means reply to; and there ended (for it was impossible it should ever be renewed) a friendship that bid fair to be lasting; being formed with a woman whose seeming stability of temper, whose knowledge of the world, and great experience of its folly, but above all, whose sense of religion, and seriousness of mind (for with all that gayety she is a great thinker), induced us both, in spite of that cautious reserve that marks our characters, to trust her, to love and value her, and to open our hearts for her reception. It may be necessary to add, that by her own desire I wrote to her under the assumed relation of a brother, and she to me as my sister. — *Ceu fumus in auras.*

I thank you for the search you have made after my intended motto, but I no longer need it. I have left myself no room for politics; that subject therefore must be postponed to a future letter. Our love is always with yourself and family. We have recovered from the concern we suffered on account of the fracas above mentioned, though for some days it made us unhappy. Not knowing but that she might possibly become sensible in a few days that she had acted hastily and unreasonably, and renew the correspondence herself, I could not in justice apprise you of this quarrel sooner; but some weeks having passed without any proposals of accommodation, I am now persuaded that none are intended, and in justice to you am obliged to caution you against a repetition of your visit.

Yours, my dear friend.

XXVII.

CONCERNING THE PREFACE TO HIS "POEMS."— LADY AUSTEN. — CONTESTED ELECTION.

To the Rev. William Unwin.

February 24, 1782.

MY DEAR FRIEND, — If I should receive a letter from you to-morrow, you must still remember that I am not in your debt, having paid you by anticipation. Knowing that you take an interest in my publication, and that you have waited for it with some impatience, I write to inform you that if it is possible for a printer to be punctual, I shall come forth on the first of March. I have ordered two copies to Stock, — one for Mr. John Unwin. It is possible, after all, that my book may come forth without a Preface. Mr. Newton has written (he could indeed write no other) a very sensible as well as a very friendly one, and it is printed. But the bookseller, who knows him well and esteems him highly, is anxious to have it cancelled, and, with my consent first obtained, has offered to negotiate that matter with the author. He judges that though it would serve to recommend the volume to the religious, it would disgust the profane, and that there is in reality no need of any Preface at all. I have found Johnson a very judicious man on other occasions, and am therefore willing that he should determine for me upon this.

Having imparted to you an account of the fracas between us and Lady Austen, it is necessary that you should be made acquainted with every event that bears any relation to that incident. The day before yesterday she sent me, by her brother-in-law, Mr. Jones, three pair of worked ruffles, with advice that I should soon receive a fourth. I knew they were begun before we quarrelled. I begged Mr. Jones to tell her when he wrote next, how much I thought myself obliged, and gave him to understand that I should make her a very inadequate, though the only return in my power, by laying my volume at her feet. This likewise she had previous reason given to expect. Thus stands the affair at present; whether anything in the shape of a reconciliation is to take place hereafter, I know not; but this I know, that when an amicable freedom of intercourse, and that unreserved confidence which belongs only to true friendship, has been once unrooted, plant it again with what care you may, it is very difficult, if not impossible, to make it grow. The fear of giving offence to a temper too apt to take it is unfavorable to that comfort we propose to ourselves even in our ordinary connections, but absolutely incompatible with the pleasures of real friendship. She is to spend the summer in our neighborhood. Lady Peterborough and Miss Mordaunt are to be of the party; the former a dissipated woman of fashion, and the latter a haughty beauty. Retirement is our passion and our delight; it is in still life alone we look for that measure of happiness we can rationally expect below. What have we to do therefore with characters like these? Shall we go to the dancing-school again? Shall we cast off the simplicity of our plain and artless demeanor, to learn, and not in a youthful day, neither, the manners of those whose manners at the best are their only recommendation, and yet can in reality recommend them to none but to people like themselves? This would be folly which nothing but necessity could excuse, and in our case no such necessity can possibly obtain. We will not go into the world; and if the world would come to us, we must give it the French answer,—*Monsieur et Madame ne sont pas visibles.*

There are but few persons to whom I present my book. The Lord Chancellor[1] is one. I enclose in a packet I send by this post to Johnson a letter to his Lordship which will accompany the volume; and to you I enclose a copy of it, because I know you will have a friendly curiosity to see it. An author is an important character. Whatever his merits may

---

[1] Edward Thurlow, formerly Cowper's fellow-clerk in a solicitor's office, now recently become Lord Chancellor. In those early days Cowper had prophesied, "I shall be always nobody, and you will be chancellor;" whereupon Thurlow had given a sportive promise to provide for his obscure friend.

be, the mere circumstance of authorship warrants his approach to persons whom otherwise perhaps he could hardly address without being deemed impertinent. He can do me no good. If I should happen to do him a little, I shall be a greater man than he. I have ordered a copy likewise to Mr. Robert Smith.

Lord Sandwich has been hard run, but I consider the push that has been made to displace him as the effort of a faction, rather than as the struggle of true patriotism convinced of his delinquency, and desirous to sacrifice him to the interests of the country. Without public virtue public prosperity cannot be long lived, and where must we look for it? It seems indeed to have a share in the motives that animate one or two of the popular party; but grant them sincere, which is a very charitable concession, the rest are evidently naught, and the quantity of salt is too small to season the mass.

I hope John continues to be pleased, and to give pleasure. If he loves instruction, he has a tutor who can give him plentifully of what he loves; and with his natural abilities his progress must be such as you would wish.

Yours.

XXVIII.

LADY AUSTEN. — SUNDAY ROUTS.

To the Rev. William Unwin.

March 7, 1782.

My dear Friend, — We have great pleasure in the contemplation of your Northern journey, as it promises us a sight of you and yours by the way, and are only sorry that Miss Shuttleworth cannot be of the party. A line to ascertain the hour when we may expect you, by the next preceding post, will be welcome.

We are far from wishing a renewal of the connection we have lately talked about. We did indeed find it in a certain way an agreeable one while that lady continued in the country, yet not altogether compatible with our favorite plan, with that silent retirement in which we have spent so many years, and in which we wish to spend what are yet before us. She is exceedingly sensible, has great quickness of parts, and an uncommon fluency of expression, but her vivacity was sometimes too much for us; occasionally perhaps it might refresh and revive us, but it more frequently exhausted us, neither your mother nor I being in that respect at all a match for her. But after all, it does not entirely depend upon us, whether our former intimacy shall take place again or not; or rather whether we shall attempt to cultivate it, or give it over, as we are most inclined to do, in despair. I suspect a little by her sending the ruffles, and by the terms in which she spoke of us to you, that some overtures on her part are to be looked for. Should this happen, however we may wish to be reserved, we must not be rude; but I can answer for us both, that we shall enter into the connection again with great reluctance, not hoping for any better fruit of it than it has already produced. If you thought she fell short of the description I gave of her, I still think however that it was not a partial one, and that it did not make too favorable a representation of her character. You *must* have seen her to a disadvantage; a consciousness of a quarrel so recent, and in which she had expressed herself with a warmth that she knew must have affronted and shocked us both, must unavoidably have produced its effect upon her behavior, which though it could not be awkward, must have been in some degree unnatural, her attention being necessarily pretty much engrossed by a recollection of what had passed between us. I would by no means have hazarded you into her company, if I had not been sure that she would treat you with politeness, and almost persuaded that she would soon see the unreasonableness of her conduct, and make a suitable apology.[1]

It is not much for my advantage that the printer delays so long to gratify your expectation. It is a state of mind that is apt to tire and disconcert us; and there are but few pleasures that make us amends for the pain of repeated disappointment. I take it for granted you have not received the volume, not

[1] Shortly after this, a reconciliation occurred, and the old easy relations were resumed.

having received it myself, nor indeed heard from Johnson, since he fixed the first of the month for its publication.

What a medley are our public prints, half the page filled with the ruin of the country, and the other half filled with the vices and pleasures of it; — here an island taken, and there a new comedy; — here an empire lost, and there an Italian opera, or the Duke of Gloucester's rout on a Sunday!

"May it please your R. H.! I am an Englishman, and must stand or fall with the nation. Religion, its true Palladium, has been stolen away; and it is crumbling into dust. Sin ruins us, the sins of the great especially, and of their sins especially the violation of the Sabbath, because it is naturally productive of all the rest. Is it fit that a Prince should make the Sabbath a day of dissipation, and that, not content with his own personal profanation of it, he should invite all whose rank entitles them to the honor of such distinction, to partake with him in his guilt? Are examples operative in proportion to the dignity of those who set them? Whose then more pernicious than your own in this flagrant instance of impiety? For shame, Sir! — if you wish well to your brother's arms, and would be glad to see the kingdom emerging again from her ruins, pay more respect to an ordinance that deserves the deepest! I do not say pardon this short remonstrance; the concern I feel for my country, and the interest I have in its prosperity, give me a right to make it. I am, etc."

Thus one might write to his Highness, and, I suppose, might be as profitably employed in whistling the tune of an old ballad. Lord P—— had a rout, too, on the same day. Is he the son of that P—— who bought Punch for a hundred pounds, and having kept him a week, tore him limb from limb because he was sullen and would not speak? Probably he is.

I have no copy of the Preface,[1] nor do I know at present how Johnson and Mr. Newton have settled it. In the matter of it there was nothing offensively peculiar. But it was thought too pious.

Yours, my dear friend.

XXIX.

THE SWEETNESS OF PRAISE FROM FRIENDS. — THE LORD CHANCELLOR'S SILENCE.

To the Rev. William Unwin.

March 18, 1782.

MY DEAR FRIEND, — Nothing has given me so much pleasure, since the publication of my volume, as your favorable opinion of it. It may possibly meet with acceptance from hundreds whose commendation would afford me no other satisfaction than what I should find in the hope that it might do them good. I have some neighbors in this place who say they like it, — doubtless I had rather they should than that they should not, — but I know them to be persons of no more taste in poetry than skill in the mathematics; their applause, therefore, is a sound that has no music in it for me. But my vanity was not so

---

[1] Written by Mr. Newton for Cowper's volume, but objected to by Johnson the publisher.

entirely quiescent when I read your friendly account of the manner in which it had affected *you*. It was tickled and pleased, and told me, in a pretty loud whisper, that others, perhaps, of whose taste and judgment I had a high opinion, would approve it too. As a giver of good counsel, I wish to please all; as an author, I am perfectly indifferent to the judgment of all except the few who are indeed judicious. The circumstance, however, in your letter which pleased me most was that you wrote in high spirits, and though you said much, suppressed more, lest you should hurt my delicacy; my delicacy is obliged to you, — but you observe it is not so squeamish but that, after it has feasted upon praise expressed, it can find a comfortable dessert in the contemplation of praise implied. I now feel as if I should be glad to begin another volume, but from the will to the power is a step too wide for me to take at present, and the season of the year brings with it so many avocations into the garden, where I am my own *factotum*, that I have little or no leisure for the quill. I should do myself much wrong, were I to omit mentioning the great complacency with which I read your narrative of Mrs. Unwin's smiles and tears. Persons of much sensibility are always persons of taste; a taste for poetry depends, indeed, upon that very article more than upon any other. If she had Aristotle by heart, I should not esteem her judgment so highly, were she defective in point of feeling, as I do and must esteem it, knowing her to have such feelings as Aristotle could not communicate, and as half the readers in the world are destitute of. This it is that makes me set so high a price upon your mother's opinion. She is a critic by nature, and not by rule, and has a perception of what is good or bad in composition that I never knew deceive her; insomuch that when two sorts of expression have pleaded equally for the preference in my own esteem, and I have referred, as in such cases I always did, the decision of the point to her, I never knew her at a loss for a just one.

Whether I shall receive any answer from his Chancellorship or not, is at present *in ambiguo*, and will probably continue in the same state of ambiguity much longer. He is so busy a man, and at this time, if the papers may be credited, so particularly busy, that I am forced to mortify myself with the thought that both my book and my letter may be thrown into a corner as too insignificant for a statesman's notice, and never found till his executor finds them. This affair, however, is neither *ad* my *libitum* nor his. I have sent him the truth, and the truth which I know he is ignorant of. He that put it into the heart of a certain Eastern monarch to amuse himself one sleepless night with listening to the records of his kingdom is able to give birth to such another occasion in Lord Thurlow's instance, and inspire him with a curiosity to know what he has received from a friend he once loved and valued. If an answer comes, however, you shall not long be a stranger to the contents of it.[1]

[1] An answer never came, nor did the great man ever take any notice of his old friend's book, — a slight greatly felt by Cowper.

I have read your letter to their Worships, and much approve of it.[1] May it have the effect it ought! If not, still you have acted an humane and becoming part, and the poor aching toes and fingers of the prisoners will not appear in judgment against you. I have made a slight alteration in the last sentence, which perhaps you will not disapprove.

Yours ever.

XXX.

ENCLOSING A LETTER FROM BENJAMIN FRANKLIN. — SPECIAL PROVIDENCES.

To the Rev. William Unwin.

May 27, 1782.

MY DEAR FRIEND, — Rather ashamed of having been at all dejected by the censure of the Critical Reviewers, who certainly could not read without prejudice a book replete with opinions and doctrines to which they cannot subscribe, I have at present no little occasion to keep a strict guard upon my vanity, lest it should be too much flattered by the following eulogium. I send it you for the reasons I gave when I imparted to you some other anecdotes of a similar kind, while we were together. Our interests in the success of this same volume are so closely united that you *must* share with me in the praise or blame that attends it; and sympathizing with me under the burden of injurious treatment, have a right to enjoy with

---

[1] A letter written by Mr Unwin to the magistrates, asking for warmer clothing for the prisoners of Chelmsford jail.

me the cordials I now and then receive, as I happen to meet with more favorable and candid judges.

A merchant, a friend of ours [1] (you will soon guess him), sent my Poems to one of the first philosophers, one of the most eminent literary characters, as well as one of the most important in the political world, that the present age can boast of. Now perhaps your conjecturing faculties are puzzled, and you begin to ask, "Who, where, and what is he? Speak out, for I am all impatience." I will not say a word more, the letter in which he returned his thanks for the present shall speak for him.

PASSY, *May* 8, 1782.

SIR, — I received the letter you did me the honor of writing to me, and am much obliged by your kind present of a book. The relish for reading of poetry had long since left me, but there is something so new in the manner, so easy and yet so correct in the language, so clear in the expression, yet concise, and so just in the sentiments, that I have read the whole with great pleasure, and some of the pieces more than once. I beg you to accept my thankful acknowledgments, and to present my respects to the author.

I shall take care to forward the letters to America, and shall be glad of any other opportunity of doing what may be agreeable to you, being with great respect for your character,

Your most obedient humble servant,

B. FRANKLIN.

We may now treat the critics as the Archbishop of Toledo treated Gil Blas, when he found fault with one of his sermons. His Grace gave him a kick, and said,

[1] Mr. John Thornton.

"Begone for a jackanapes, and furnish yourself with a better taste, if you know where to find it."

We are glad that you are safe at home again. Could we see at one glance of the eye what is passing every day upon all the roads in the kingdom, how many are terrified and hurt, how many plundered and abused, we should indeed find reason enough to be thankful for journeys performed in safety, and for deliverance from dangers we are not perhaps even permitted to see. When in some of the high southern latitudes and in a dark tempestuous night a flash of lightning discovered to Captain Cook a vessel, which glanced along close by his side, and which but for the lightning he must have run foul of, both the danger and the transient light that showed it were undoubtedly designed to convey to him this wholesome instruction, — that a particular Providence attended him, and that he was not only preserved from evils of which he had notice, but from many more of which he had no information, or even the least suspicion. What unlikely contingencies may nevertheless take place! How improbable that two ships should dash against each other, in the midst of the vast Pacific Ocean, and that steering contrary courses from parts of the world so immensely distant from each other, they should yet move so exactly in a line as to clash, fill, and go to the bottom, in a sea where all the ships in the world might be so dispersed as that none should see another! Yet this must have happened but for the remarkable interference which he has recorded. The same Providence indeed might as easily have conducted them so wide of each other that they should never have met at all; but then this lesson would have been lost; at least, the heroic voyager would have encompassed the globe without having had occasion to relate an incident that so naturally suggests it.

I am no more delighted with the season than you are. The absence of the sun, which has graced the spring with much less of his presence than he vouchsafed to the winter, has a very uncomfortable effect upon my frame. I feel an invincible aversion to employment, which I am yet constrained to fly to as my only remedy against something worse. If I do nothing, I am dejected; if I do anything, I am weary; and that weariness is best described by the word "lassitude," which is of all weariness in the world the most oppressive. But enough of myself and the weather.

The blow we have struck in the West Indies[1] will, I suppose, be decisive at least for the present year, and so far as that part of our possessions is concerned in the present conflict. But the news-writers and their correspondents disgust me, and make me sick. One victory after such a long series of adverse occurrences has filled them with self-conceit and impertinent boasting; and while Rodney is almost accounted a Methodist for ascribing his success to Providence, men who have renounced all dependence upon such a friend, without whose assistance nothing can be done, threaten to drive the French out of the sea, laugh at the Spaniards, sneer at the Dutch, and are to carry the world before them. Our enemies are apt to brag, and we deride them for it; but we can sing as loud as they can, in the same key, and no doubt

[1] An allusion to the victory gained by Sir George Rodney over Count de Grasse, April 12, 1782.

wherever our papers go, shall be derided in our turn. An Englishman's true glory should be to do his business well and say little about it; but he disgraces himself when he puffs his prowess as if he had finished his task, when he has but just begun it.

Yours.

XXXI.

AMBITIONS IN REGARD TO AN OLNEY REPUTATION.

To the Rev. William Unwin.

June 12, 1782.

MY DEAR FRIEND, — Every extraordinary occurrence in our lives affords us an opportunity to learn, if we will, something more of our own hearts and tempers than we are aware of. It is easy to promise ourselves beforehand that our conduct shall be wise or moderate or resolute on any given occasion. But when that occasion occurs, we do not always find it easy to make good the promise, — such a difference there is between theory and practice. Perhaps this is no new remark; but it is not a whit the worse for being old, if it be true.

Before I had published, I said to myself: You and I, Mr. Cowper, will not concern ourselves much about what the critics may say of our book. But having once sent my wits for a venture, I soon became anxious about the issue, and found that I could not be satisfied with a warm place in my own good graces, unless my friends were pleased with me as much as I pleased myself. Meeting with their approbation, I began to feel the workings of ambition. It is well, said I, that my friends are pleased ; but friends are sometimes partial, and mine, I have reason to think, are not altogether free from bias : methinks I should like to hear a stranger or two speak well of me. I was presently gratified by the approbation of the London Magazine, and the Gentleman's, particularly by that of the former, and by the plaudit of Dr. Franklin. By the way, magazines are publications we have but little respect for, till we ourselves are chronicled in them, and then they assume an importance in our esteem which before we could not allow them. But the Monthly Review, the most formidable of all my judges, is still behind. What will that critical Rhadamanthus say, when my shivering genius shall appear before him? Still he keeps me in hot water, and I must wait another month for his award. Alas! when I wish for a favorable sentence from that quarter (to confess a weakness that I should not confess to all), I feel myself not a little influenced by a tender regard to my reputation here, even among my neighbors at Olney. Here are watchmakers, who themselves are wits, and who at present perhaps think me one. Here is a carpenter and a baker, and, not to mention others, here is your idol Mr. Teedon, whose smile is fame. All these read the Monthly Review, and all these will set me down for a dunce, if those terrible critics show them the example. But oh! wherever else I am accounted dull, dear Mr. Griffith, let me pass for a genius at Olney!

XXXII.

OLNEY CHARITIES — JOHN GILPIN.

To the Rev. William Unwin.

November 18, 1782.

MY DEAR WILLIAM, — On the part of the poor, and on our part, be pleased to make acknowledgments such as the occasion calls for to our beneficent friend Mr. Smith.[1] I call him ours, because having experienced his kindness to myself in a former instance, and in the present his disinterested readiness to succor the distressed, my ambition will be satisfied with nothing less. He may depend upon the strictest secrecy; no creature shall hear him mentioned, either now or hereafter, as the person from whom we have received this bounty. But when I speak of him, or hear him spoken of by others, which sometimes happens, I shall not forget what is due to so rare a character. I wish, and your mother wishes it too, that he could sometimes take us in his way to Nottingham; he will find us happy to receive a person whom we must needs account it an honor to know. We shall exercise our best discretion in the disposal of the money; but in this town, where the gospel has been preached so many years, where the people have been favored so long with laborious and conscientious ministers, it is not an easy thing to find those who make no profession of religion at all, and are yet proper objects of charity. The profane are so profane, so drunken,

[1] Afterward Lord Carrington.

dissolute, and in every respect worthless, that to make them partakers of his bounty would be to abuse it. We promise, however, that none shall touch it but such as are miserably poor, yet at the same time industrious and honest, — two characters frequently united here, where the most watchful and unremitting labor will hardly procure them bread. We make none but the cheapest laces, and the price of them is fallen almost to nothing. Thanks are due to yourself likewise, and are hereby accordingly rendered, for waiving your claim in behalf of your own parishioners. You are always with them, and they are always, at least some of them, the better for your residence among them. Olney is a populous place, inhabited chiefly by the half-starved and the ragged of the earth, and it is not possible for our small party and small ability to extend their operations so far as to be much felt among such numbers. Accept therefore your share of their gratitude, and be convinced that when they pray for a blessing upon those who have relieved their wants, He that answers that prayer, and when he answers it, will remember his servant at Stock.

I little thought, when I was writing the history of John Gilpin, that he would appear in print. I intended to laugh, and to make two or three others laugh, of whom you were one. But now all the world laughs, at least if they have the same relish for a tale ridiculous in itself, and quaintly told, as we have. Well, they do not always laugh so innocently or at so small an expense, — for in a world like this, abounding with subjects for satire, and with satirical wits to mark them, a laugh that hurts nobody has at least the grace of novelty to recommend it. Swift's darling motto was, *Vive la bagatelle,* — a good wish for a philosopher of his complexion, the greater part of whose wisdom, whencesoever it came, most certainly came not from above. *La bagatelle* has no enemy in me, though it has neither so warm a friend nor so able a one as it had in him. If I trifle, and merely trifle, it is because I am reduced to it by necessity, — a melancholy, that nothing else so effectually disperses, engages me sometimes in the arduous task of being merry by force. And, strange as it may seem, the most ludicrous lines I ever wrote have been written in the saddest mood, and, but for that saddest mood, perhaps had never been written at all.[1] To say truth, it would be but a shocking vagary, should the mariners on board a ship buffeted by a terrible storm employ themselves in fiddling and dancing; yet sometimes much such a part act I.

I hear from Mrs. Newton that some great persons have spoken with great approbation of a certain book. Who they are, and what they have said, I am to be told in a future letter. The Monthly Reviewers in the mean time have satisfied me well enough. Yours, my dear William.

[1] The story of John Gilpin was told to Cowper by Lady Austen, as she had heard it in her childhood, on an afternoon when he had appeared more than usually depressed. The next morning he said to her that he had been kept awake during the greater part of the night by thinking of the story and laughing at it, and that he had turned it into a ballad. The ballad was sent to Mr. Unwin, who had it printed in the "Public Advertiser;" Cowper little anticipated what a race of popularity the famous horseman was to run.

XXXIII.

A GROUP OF OLNEY POLITICIANS. — ENGLAND IN THE AMERICAN WAR MORE SINNED AGAINST THAN SINNING.

To the Rev. John Newton.

January 26, 1783.

MY DEAR FRIEND, — It is reported among persons of the best intelligence at Olney — the barber, the schoolmaster, and the drummer of a corps quartered at this place — that the belligerent powers are at last reconciled, the articles of the treaty adjusted, and that peace is at the door. I saw this morning, at nine o'clock, a group of about twelve figures very closely engaged in a conference, as I suppose, upon the same subject. The scene of consultation was a blacksmith's shed, very comfortably screened from the wind, and directly opposed to the morning sun. Some held their hands behind them, some had them folded across their bosom, and others had thrust them into their breeches pockets. Every man's posture bespoke a pacific turn of mind; but the distance being too great for their words to reach me, nothing transpired. I am willing, however, to hope that the secret will not be a secret long, and that you and I, equally interested in the event, though not perhaps equally well-informed, shall soon have an opportunity to rejoice in the completion of it. The powers of Europe have clashed with each other to a fine purpose;[1] that the Americans, at length declared in-

[1] France, Spain, and Holland, all of whom united with America against England.

dependent, may keep themselves so, if they can ; and that what the parties who have thought proper to dispute upon that point have wrested from each other in the course of the conflict may be, in the issue of it, restored to the proper owner. Nations may be guilty of a conduct that would render an individual infamous forever, and yet carry their heads high, talk of their glory, and despise their neighbors. Your opinions and mine, I mean our political ones, are not exactly of a piece, yet I cannot think otherwise upon this subject than I have always done. England, more perhaps through the fault of her generals than her councils, has in some instances acted with a spirit of cruel animosity she was never chargeable with till now. But this is the worst that can be said. On the other hand, the Americans, who, if they had contented themselves with a struggle for lawful liberty, would have deserved applause, seem to me to have incurred the guilt of parricide, by renouncing their parent, by making her ruin their favorite object, and by associating themselves with their worst enemy, for the accomplishment of their purpose. France, and of course Spain, have acted a treacherous, a thievish part. They have stolen America from England ; and whether they are able to possess themselves of that jewel or not hereafter, it was doubtless what they intended. Holland appears to me in a meaner light than any of them. They quarrelled with a friend for an enemy's sake. The French led them by the nose, and the English have thrashed them for suffering it. My views of the contest being, and having been always such, I have consequently brighter hopes for England than her situation some time since seemed to justify. She is the only injured party. America may, perhaps, call her the aggressor; but if she were so, America has not only repelled the injury, but done a greater. As to the rest, if perfidy, treachery, avarice, and ambition can prove their cause to have been a rotten one, those proofs are found upon them. I think, therefore, that whatever scourge may be prepared for England on some future day, her ruin is not yet to be expected.

Acknowledge, now, that I am worthy of a place under the shed I described, and that I should make no small figure among the *quidnuncs* of Olney.

I wish the society you have formed may prosper.[1] Your subjects will be of greater importance, and discussed with more sufficiency. The earth is a grain of sand, but the spiritual interests of man are commensurate with the heavens.

Pray remind Mr. Bull, who has too much genius to have a good memory, that he has an account to settle for Mrs. Unwin with her grocer, and give our love to him. Accept for yourself and Mrs. Newton your just share of the same commodity, with our united thanks for a very fine barrel of oysters. This, indeed, is rather commending the barrel than its contents. I should say, therefore, for a barrel of very fine oysters.

Yours, my dear friend, as ever.

[1] The Eclectic Society, consisting of Newton, Scott, Cecil, Foster, and other ministers, who met at stated intervals for mental edification.

XXXIV.

RESTORATION OF FRIENDSHIP BETWEEN THE KINGS OF ENGLAND AND FRANCE.

To the Rev. William Unwin.

February 2, 1783.

I GIVE you joy of the restoration of that sincere and firm friendship between the Kings of England and France that has been so long interrupted. It is great pity when hearts so cordially united are divided by trifles. Thirteen pitiful colonies, which the King of England chose to keep and the King of France to obtain if he could, have disturbed that harmony which would else, no doubt, have subsisted between those illustrious personages to this moment. If the King of France, whose greatness of mind is only equalled by that of his Queen, had regarded them, unworthy of his notice as they were, with an eye of suitable indifference; or had he thought it a matter deserving in any degree his princely attention, that they were, in reality, the property of his good friend the King of England; or had the latter been less obstinately determined to hold fast his interest in them; and could he, with that civility and politeness in which monarchs are expected to excel, have entreated his Majesty of France to accept a bagatelle, for which he seemed to have conceived so strong a predilection, all this mischief had been prevented. But monarchs, alas! crowned and sceptred as they are, are yet but men; they fall out and are reconciled, just like the meanest of their subjects. I cannot, however, sufficiently admire the moderation and magnanimity of the King of England. His dear friend on the other side of the Channel has not, indeed, taken actual possession of the colonies in question, but he has effectually wrested them out of the hands of their original owner; who, nevertheless, letting fall the extinguisher of patience upon the flame of his resentment, and glowing with no other flame than that of the sincerest affection, embraces the King of France again, gives him Senegal and Goree in Africa, gives him the islands he had taken from him in the West, gives him his conquered territories in the East, gives him a fishery upon the banks of Newfoundland; and, as if all this were too little, merely because he knows that Louis has a partiality for the King of Spain, gives to the latter an island in the Mediterranean which thousands of English had purchased with their lives, and in America all that he wanted, — at least, all that he could ask. No doubt there will be great cordiality between this royal trio for the future; and though wars may perhaps be kindled between their posterity some ages hence, the present generation shall never be witnesses of such a calamity again. I expect soon to hear that the Queen of France, who just before this rupture happened made the Queen of England a present of a watch, has, in acknowledgment of all these acts of kindness, sent her also a seal wherewith to ratify the treaty. Surely she can do no less.

XXXV.

REFLECTIONS ON THE PEACE.

To the Rev. John Newton.

February 8, 1783.

MY DEAR FRIEND, — When I contemplate the nations of the earth, and their conduct towards each other, through the medium of scriptural light, my opinions of them are exactly like your own. Whether they do good or do evil, I see them acting under the permission or direction of that Providence who governs the earth, whose operations are as irresistible as they are silent and unsuspected. So far we are perfectly agreed; and howsoever we may differ upon inferior parts of the subject, it is, as you say, an affair of no great consequence. For instance, you think the peace a better than we deserve, and in a certain sense I agree with you: as a sinful nation we deserve no peace at all, and have reason enough to be thankful that the voice of war is at any rate put to silence. But when I consider the peace as the work of our ministers, and reflect that with more wisdom or more spirit they might perhaps have procured a better, I confess it does not please me. Such another peace would ruin us, I suppose, as effectually as a war protracted to the extremest inch of our ability to bear it. I do not think it just that the French should plunder us and be paid for doing it, nor does it appear to me that there was an absolute necessity for such tameness on our part as we discover in the present treaty. We give away all that is demanded, and receive nothing but what was our own before. So far as this stain upon our national honor and this diminution of our national property are a judgment upon our iniquities, I submit, and have no doubt but that ultimately it will be found to be judgment mixed with mercy. But so far as I see it to be the effect of French knavery and British despondency, I feel it as a disgrace, and grumble at it as a wrong. I dislike it the more, because the peacemaker has been so immoderately praised for his performance, which is, in my opinion, a contemptible one enough. Had he made the French smart for their baseness, I would have praised him too, — a minister should have shown his wisdom by securing some points, at least, for the benefit of his country. A schoolboy might have made concessions. After all, perhaps, the worst consequence of this awkward business will be dissension in the two Houses, and dissatisfaction throughout the kingdom. They that love their country will be grieved to see her trampled upon, and they that love mischief will have a fair opportunity of making it. Were I a member of the Commons, even with the same religious sentiments as impress me now, I should think it my duty to condemn it.

You will suppose me a politician; but in truth I am nothing less. These are the thoughts that occur to me while I read the newspaper; and when I have laid it down, I feel myself more interested in the success of my early cucumbers than in any part of this great and important subject. If I see them droop a little, I forget that we have been many years at war, that we have made a humiliating peace,[1] that we are deeply in debt and unable to pay. All these reflections are absorbed at once in the anxiety I feel for a plant the fruit of which I cannot eat when I have procured it. How wise, how consistent, how respectable a creature is man!

Because we have nobody to preach the gospel at Olney, Mr. Chater waits only for a barn, at present occupied by a strolling company; and the moment they quit it, he begins. He is disposed to think the dissatisfied of all denominations may possibly be united under his standard, and that the great work of forming a more extensive and more established interest than any of them is reserved for him.

Mrs. Unwin thanks Mrs. Newton for her kind letter and for executing her commissions. She means to answer next week by the opportunity of a basket of chickens. We truly love you both, think of you often, and one of us prays for you; the other will when he can pray for himself.

---

[1] Lord Shelburne, who made this peace, was taunted for it in the House of Commons by Mr. Fox. His defence was that he was compelled to the measure, and not so much the author as the instrument of it.

XXXVI.

DOUBTS CONCERNING THE FUTURE PROSPECTS OF AMERICA.

To the Rev. John Newton.

February 24, 1783.

MY DEAR FRIEND, — A weakness in one of my eyes may possibly shorten my letter, but I mean to make it as long as my present materials and my ability to write can suffice for.

I am almost sorry to say that I am reconciled to the peace, being reconciled to it not upon principles of approbation but necessity. The deplorable condition of the country, insisted on by the friends of administration, and not denied by their adversaries, convinces me that our only refuge under Heaven was in the treaty with which I quarrelled. The treaty itself I find less objectionable than I did, Lord Shelburne having given a color to some of the articles that makes them less painful in the contemplation. But my opinion upon the whole affair is, that now is the time (if indeed there is salvation for the country) for Providence to interpose to save it. A peace with the greatest political advantages would not have healed us; a peace with none may procrastinate our ruin for a season, but cannot ultimately prevent it. The prospect may make all tremble who have no trust in God, and even they that trust may tremble. The peace will probably be of short duration, and, in the ordinary course of things, another war must end us. A great country in ruins will not be beheld with eyes of indifference, even by those who have a better country to look to. But with them all will be well at last.

As to the Americans, perhaps I do not forgive them as I ought; perhaps I shall always think of them with some resentment as the destroyers, intentionally the destroyers, of this country. They have pushed that point farther than the house of Bourbon could have carried it in half a century. I may be prejudiced against them, but I do not think them equal to the task of establishing an empire. Great men are necessary for such a purpose; and their great men, I believe, are yet unborn. They have had passion and obstinacy enough to do us much mischief; but whether the event will be salutary to themselves or not, must wait for proof. I agree with you that it is possible America may become a land of extraordinary evangelical light; but at the same time I cannot discover anything in their new situation peculiarly favorable to such a supposition. They cannot have more liberty of conscience than they had; at least, if that liberty was under any restraint, it was a restraint of their own making. Perhaps a new settlement in Church and State may leave them less. Well, all will be over soon. The time is at hand when an empire will be established that shall fill the earth. Neither statesmen nor generals will lay the foundation of it, but it shall rise at the sound of the trumpet.

Mr. Scott's last child is dead, — died this morning at four o'clock. The great blemish it had in its face made it a desirable thing that it should not live; and a virulent humor, which consumed the flesh from the bones, made it desirable that it should die soon. It lived a little time in a world of which it knew nothing, and is gone to another in which it is already become wiser than the wisest it has left behind.

Our united thanks both for the worsted and the satin; they are remarkably well dyed. The former arrived in the shape of a pair of breeches.

I am well in body, but with a mind that would wear out a frame of adamant; yet upon *my* frame, which is not very robust, its effects are not discernible. Mrs. Unwin is in health. Accept our unalienable love to you both.

Yours, my dear friend, truly.

XXXVII.

AMERICAN LOYALISTS. — PROSPECTS OF THE UNITED STATES.

To the Rev. John Newton.

October, 1783.

My dear Friend, — I am much obliged to you for your American anecdotes, and feel the obligation perhaps more sensibly, the labor of transcribing being in particular that to which I myself have the greatest aversion. The Loyalists are much to be pitied;[1] driven from all the comforts that depend upon and are intimately connected with a residence in their native land, and sent to cultivate a distant one, without the means of doing it; abandoned too, through a deplorable necessity, by the government to which

[1] Being persecuted by America, and neglected by England.

they have sacrificed all, — they exhibit a spectacle of distress which one cannot view even at this distance without participating in what they feel. Why could not some of our useless wastes and forests have been allotted to their support? To have built them houses indeed, and to have furnished them with implements of husbandry, would have put us to no small expense; but I suppose the increase of population and the improvement of the soil would soon have been felt as a national advantage, and have indemnified the State, if not enriched it. But I am afraid that nothing so virtuous or so wise is to be looked for in the public measures of the present day. We are bountiful to foreigners, and neglect those of our own household. I remember that, compassionating the miseries of the Portuguese, at the time of the Lisbon earthquake, we sent them a ship-load of tools to clear away the rubbish with, and to assist them in rebuilding the city. I remember, too, it was reported at the time that the court of Portugal accepted our wheelbarrows and spades with a very ill grace, and treated our bounty with contempt. An act like this in behalf of our brethren, carried only a little further, might possibly have redeemed them from ruin, have resulted in emolument to ourselves, have been received with joy, and repaid with gratitude. Such are my speculations upon the subject, who not being a politician by profession, and very seldom giving my attention for a moment to any such matter, may not be aware of difficulties and objections which they of the cabinet can discern with half an eye. Perhaps to have taken under our protection a race of men proscribed by the Congress might be thought dangerous to the interests we hope to have hereafter in their high and mighty regards and affections. It is ever the way of those who rule the earth, to leave out of their reckoning Him who rules the universe. They forget that the poor have a friend more powerful to avenge than they can be to oppress, and that treachery and perfidy must therefore prove bad policy in the end. The Americans themselves appear to me to be in a situation little less pitiable than that of the deserted Loyalists. A revolt can hardly be said to have been successful that has exchanged only an apprehended tyranny for a real one, and has shaken off the restraints of a well-ordered government, merely to give room and opportunity for the jarring opinions and interests of its abetters to throw all into a state of anarchy. This is evidently the case at present, and without a special interposition of Providence is likely to be for years to come. They will at last, perhaps, after much ill temper and bloodshed, settle into some sort of establishment; but hardly, I think, into a more desirable one (and it seems they themselves are pretty much of the same opinion) than they enjoyed before. Their fears of arbitrary imposition were certainly well founded. A struggle therefore might be necessary, in order to prevent it, and this end might surely have been answered without a renunciation of dependence. But the passions of a whole people, once put in motion, are not soon quieted. Contest begets aversion, a little success inspires more ambitious hopes, and thus a slight quarrel terminates at last in a breach never to be healed, and perhaps in the ruin of both parties. It does not seem likely that a country so distinguished by the Creator with everything that can make it desirable should be given up to desolation forever, and they possibly may have reason on their side who suppose that in time it will have the pre-eminence over all others; but the day of such prosperity seems far distant: Omnipotence indeed can hasten it, and it may dawn when it is least expected. But we govern ourselves in all our reasonings by present appearances. Persons at least no better informed than myself are constrained to do so.

You surprised me most agreeably with a polite and sensible letter from Mr. Bacon;[1] that good man has a place in my heart, though I never saw him and never may. I shall never see the print he so obligingly presents me with, without sentiments of gratitude and friendship, and shall endeavor to answer his letter in such terms as his kindness justly claims, as soon as the print arrives.

We have opened two of the cocoanuts,— one naught and the other excellent; the third promises to be a good one. I intended to have taken another subject when I began, and I wish I had. No man living is less qualified to settle nations than I am; but when I write to you, I talk, — that is, I write as fast as my pen can run, and on this occasion it ran away with

---

[1] The sculptor of Lord Chatham's monument, and thus alluded to in "The Task":—

"Bacon there
Gives more than female beauty to a stone,
And Chatham's eloquence to marble lips." — *Book I.*

me. I acknowledge myself in your debt for your last favor, but cannot pay you now, unless you will accept as payment what I know you value more than all I can say beside, the most unfeigned assurances of my affection for you and yours.

Yours, etc.

XXXVIII.

OLNEY NEWS. — ANTICIPATIONS OF BALLOON TRAVELLING.

To the Rev. John Newton.

November 17, 1783.

MY DEAR FRIEND, — A parcel arrived last night, the contents of which shall be disposed of according to order. We thank Mrs. Newton (not from the teeth outwards) for the tooth-brushes.

The country around us is much alarmed with apprehensions of fire. Two have happened since that of Olney, — one at Hitchin, where the damage is said to amount to eleven thousand pounds; and another at a place not far from Hitchin, of which I have not learned the name. Letters have been dropped at Bedford, threatening to burn the town; and the inhabitants have been so intimidated as to have placed a guard in many parts of it, several nights past. Some madman or some devil has broke loose, who it is to be hoped will pay dear for these effusions of his malignity. Since our conflagration here, we have sent two women and a boy to the justice, for depredation, — Sue Riviss, for stealing a piece of beef, which, in her excuse, she said she intended to take care of. This lady, whom you well remember, escaped for want of evidence; not that evidence was indeed wanting, but our men of Gotham judged it unnecessary to send it. With her went the woman I mentioned before, who it seems has made some sort of profession, but upon this occasion allowed herself a latitude of conduct rather inconsistent with it, having filled her apron with wearing apparel, which she likewise intended to take care of. She would have gone to the county jail, had Billy Raban, the baker's son, who prosecuted, insisted upon it; but he good-naturedly, though I think weakly, interposed in her favor, and begged her off. The young gentleman who accompanied these fair ones is the junior son of Molly Boswell. He had stolen some iron-work, the property of Griggs, the butcher. Being convicted, he was ordered to be whipped, which operation he underwent at the cart's tail, from the stone-house to the high arch, and back again. He seemed to show great fortitude, but it was all an imposition upon the public. The beadle, who performed, had filled his left hand with red ochre, through which after every stroke he drew the lash of his whip, leaving the appearance of a wound upon the skin, but in reality not hurting him at all. This being perceived by Mr. Constable Hinschcomb, who followed the beadle, he applied his cane, without any such management or precaution, to the shoulders of the too-merciful executioner. The scene immediately became more interesting. The beadle could by no means be prevailed upon to strike hard, which provoked the constable to strike harder; and this double flogging continued till a lass of Silver-end, pitying the pitiful beadle thus suffering under the hands of the pitiless constable, joined the procession, and placing herself immediately behind the latter, seized him by his capillary club, and pulling him backwards by the same, slapped his face with a most Amazonian fury. This concatenation of events has taken up more of my paper than I intended it should, but I could not forbear to inform you how the beadle thrashed the thief, the constable the beadle, and the lady the constable, and how the thief was the only person concerned who suffered nothing. Mr. Teedon[1] has been here, and is gone again. He came to thank me for an old pair of breeches. In answer to our inquiries after his health, he replied that he had a slow fever, which made him take all possible care not to inflame his blood. I admitted his prudence, but in his particular instance could not very clearly discern the need of it. Pump water will not heat him much; and, to speak a little in his own style, more inebriating fluids are to him, I fancy, not very attainable. He brought us news, the truth of which, however, I do not vouch for, that the town of Bedford was actually on fire yesterday, and the flames not extinguished when the bearer of the tidings left it.

Swift observes, when he is giving his reasons why

[1] A poor schoolmaster at Olney, and one of Cowper's pensioners.

the preacher is elevated always above his hearers, that let the crowd be as great as it will below, there is always room enough overhead. If the French philosophers can carry their art of flying to the perfection they desire, the observation may be reversed, the crowd will be overhead, and they will have most room who stay below. I can assure you, however, upon my own experience, that this way of travelling is very delightful. I dreamed, a night or two since, that I drove myself through the upper regions in a balloon and pair, with the greatest ease and security. Having finished the tour I intended, I made a short turn, and with one flourish of my whip descended; my horses prancing and curvetting with an infinite share of spirit, but without the least danger, either to me or my vehicle. The time, we may suppose, is at hand, and seems to be prognosticated by my dream, when these airy excursions will be universal, when judges will fly the circuit, and bishops their visitations; and when the tour of Europe will be performed with much greater speed, and with equal advantage, by all who travel merely for the sake of having it to say that they have made it.[1]

I beg you will accept for yourself and yours our unfeigned love, and remember me affectionately to Mr. Bacon when you see him.

Yours, my dear friend.

[1] Balloons were a new thing at this time, and **were** attracting much attention and many speculations **from the public.**

XXXIX.

FIRST INTRODUCTION TO THE THROCKMORTONS.

To the Rev. William Unwin.

My dear Friend, — It is hard upon us striplings who have uncles still living (N. B. I myself have an uncle still alive), that those venerable gentlemen should stand in our way, even when the ladies are in question; that I, for instance, should find in one page of your letter a hope that Miss Shuttleworth would be of your party, and be told in the next that she is engaged to your uncle. Well, we may perhaps never be uncles; but we may reasonably hope that the time is coming when others, as young as we are now, shall envy us the privileges of old age, and see us engross that share in the attention of the ladies to which their youth must aspire in vain. Make our compliments if you please to your sister Elizabeth, and tell her that we are both mortified at having missed the pleasure of seeing her.

Balloons are so much the mode that even in this country we have attempted a balloon. You may possibly remember that at a place called Weston, little more than a mile from Olney, there lives a family whose name is Throckmorton. The present possessor of the estate is a young man whom I remember a boy. He has a wife, who is young, genteel, and handsome. They are Papists, but much more amiable than many Protestants. We never had any intercourse with the family, though ever since we lived here we have enjoyed the range of their pleasure-grounds, having been favored with a key which admits us into all. When this man succeeded to the estate, on the death of his elder brother, and came to settle at Weston, I sent him a complimentary card, requesting the continuance of that privilege, having till then enjoyed it by the favor of his mother, who on that occasion went to finish her days at Bath. You may conclude that he granted it, and for about two years nothing more passed between us. A fortnight ago, I received an invitation in the civilest terms, in which he told me that the next day he should attempt to fill a balloon, and if it would be any pleasure to me to be present, should be happy to see me. Your mother and I went. The whole country were there, but the balloon could not be filled. The endeavor was, I believe, very philosophically made; but such a process depends for its success upon such niceties as make it very precarious. Our reception was however flattering to a great degree, insomuch that more notice seemed to be taken of us than we could possibly have expected; indeed, rather more than of any of his other guests. They even seemed anxious to recommend themselves to our regards. We drank chocolate, and were asked to dine, but were engaged. A day or two afterwards, Mrs. Unwin and I walked that way, and were overtaken in a shower. I found a tree that I thought would shelter us both, — a large elm, in a grove that fronts the mansion. Mrs. T. observed us, and running towards us in the rain, insisted on our walking in. He was gone out. We sat chatting with her till the weather cleared up, and then at her instance took a walk with her in the garden. The garden is almost their only walk, and is certainly their only retreat in which they are not liable to interruption. She offered us a key of it in a manner that made it impossible not to accept it, and said she would send us one. A few days afterwards, in the cool of the evening, we walked that way again. We saw them going toward the house, and exchanged bows and courtesies at a little distance, but did not join them. In a few minutes, when we had passed the house, and had almost reached the gate that opens out of the park into the adjoining field, I heard the iron gate belonging to the courtyard ring, and saw Mr. T. advancing hastily toward us; we made equal haste to meet him, he presented to us the key, which I told him I esteemed a singular favor, and after a few such speeches as are made on such occasions, we parted. This happened about a week ago. I concluded nothing less than that all this civility and attention was designed, on their part, as a prelude to a nearer acquaintance; but here at present the matter rests. I should like exceedingly to be on an easy footing there, to give a morning call and now and then to receive one, but nothing more. For though he is one of the most agreeable men I ever saw, I could not wish to visit him in any other way, neither our house, furniture, servants, nor income being such as qualify us to make entertainments; neither would I on any account be introduced to the neighboring gentry, which must be the consequence of our dining there, there not being a man in the country, except himself, with whom I could endure to associate. They are squires, merely such, purse-proud and sportsmen. But Mr. T. is altogether a man of fashion, and respectable on every account.

I have told you a long story. Farewell. We number the days as they pass, and are glad that we shall see you and your sister soon.

Yours, etc.

XL.

VISIT FROM A CANDIDATE.

To the Rev. John Newton.

March 29, 1784.

MY DEAR FRIEND, — It being his Majesty's pleasure that I should yet have another opportunity to write before he dissolves the parliament, I avail myself of it with all possible alacrity. I thank you for your last, which was not the less welcome for coming, like an extraordinary gazette, at a time when it was not expected.

As when the sea is uncommonly agitated the water finds its way into creeks and holes of rocks which in its calmer state it never reaches, in like manner the effect of these turbulent times is felt even at Orchard side, where in general we live as undisturbed by the political element as shrimps or cockles that have been accidentally deposited in some hollow beyond the water-mark, by the usual dashing of the waves. We were sitting yesterday after dinner, the two ladies and myself, very composedly, and without the least apprehension of any such intrusion in our snug parlor, one lady knitting, the other netting, and the gentleman winding worsted, when to our unspeakable surprise a mob appeared before the window; a smart rap was heard at the door, the boys hallooed, and the maid announced Mr. Grenville. Puss[1] was unfortunately let out of her box, so that the candidate, with all his good friends at his heels, was refused admittance at the grand entry, and referred to the back door, as the only possible way of approach.

Candidates are creatures not very susceptible of affronts, and would rather, I suppose, climb in at a window than be absolutely excluded. In a minute the yard, the kitchen, and the parlor were filled. Mr. Grenville, advancing toward me, shook me by the hand with a degree of cordiality that was extremely seducing. As soon as he and as many more as could find chairs were seated, he began to open the intent of his visit. I told him I had no vote, for which he readily gave me credit. I assured him I had no influence, which he was not equally inclined to believe, and the less, no doubt, because Mr. Ashburner, the draper, addressing himself to me at this moment, informed me that I had a great deal. Supposing that I could not be possessed of such a treasure without knowing it, I ventured to confirm my first assertion, by saying that if I had any I was utterly at a loss to imagine where it could be, or wherein it consisted. Thus ended the conference. Mr. Grenville squeezed me by the hand again, kissed the

[1] His tame hare.

ladies, and withdrew. He kissed likewise the maid in the kitchen, and seemed upon the whole a most loving, kissing, kind-hearted gentleman. He is very young, genteel, and handsome. He has a pair of very good eyes in his head, which not being sufficient as it should seem for the many nice and difficult purposes of a senator, he has a third also, which he wore suspended by a riband from his buttonhole. The boys hallooed, the dogs barked, Puss scampered; the hero, with his long train of obsequious followers, withdrew. We made ourselves very merry with the adventure, and in a short time settled into our former tranquillity, never probably to be thus interrupted more. I thought myself, however, happy in being able to affirm truly that I had not that influence for which he sued, and which, had I been possessed of it, with my present views of the dispute between the Crown and the Commons, I must have refused him, for he is on the side of the former. It is comfortable to be of no consequence in a world where one cannot exercise any without disobliging somebody. The town, however, seems to be much at his service, and if he be equally successful throughout the county he will undoubtedly gain his election. Mr. Ashburner perhaps was a little mortified, because it was evident that I owed the honor of this visit to his misrepresentation of my importance. But had he thought proper to assure Mr. Grenville that I had three heads, I should not, I suppose, have been bound to produce them.

Mr. Scott,[1] who you say was so much admired in

[1] Mr. Newton's successor in Olney.

your pulpit, would be equally admired in his own, at least by all capable judges, were he not so apt to be angry with his congregation. This hurts him, and had he the understanding and eloquence of Paul himself, would still hurt him. He seldom, hardly ever indeed, preaches a gentle, well-tempered sermon, but I hear it highly commended; but warmth of temper, indulged to a degree that may be called scolding, defeats the end of preaching. It is a misapplication of his powers, which it also cripples, and teases away his hearers. But he is a good man, and may perhaps outgrow it.

Many thanks for the worsted, which is excellent. We are as well as a spring hardly less severe than the severest winter will give us leave to be. With our united love, we conclude ourselves yours and Mrs. Newton's affectionate and faithful

W. C.
M. U.

XLI.

ON BEATTIE; BLAIR; THE ORIGIN OF LANGUAGE.

To the Rev. William Unwin.

April 5, 1784.

MY DEAR WILLIAM, — The hat which I desired you to procure for me, I now write to desire that you will not procure. Do not hastily infer that I mean to go about bareheaded: the whole of the matter is that a readier method of supply has presented itself since I wrote.

I thanked you in my last for Johnson; I now thank you with more emphasis for Beattie, the most agreeable and amiable writer I ever met with, — the only author I have seen whose critical and philosophical researches are diversified and embellished by a poetical imagination that makes even the driest subject and the leanest a feast for an epicure in books. He is so much at his ease, too, that his own character appears in every page, and, which is very rare, we see not only the writer, but the man; and that man so gentle, so well-tempered, so happy in his religion, and so humane in his philosophy that it is necessary to love him, if one has the least sense of what is lovely. If you have not his poem called "The Minstrel," and cannot borrow it, I must beg you to buy it for me; for though I cannot afford to deal largely in so expensive a commodity as books, I must afford to purchase at least the poetical works of Beattie.

I have read six of Blair's lectures, and what do I say of Blair? That he is a sensible man, master of his subject, and excepting here and there a Scotticism, a good writer, so far at least as perspicuity of expression and method contribute to make one. But oh, the sterility of that man's fancy! if indeed he has any such faculty belonging to him. Perhaps philosophers, or men designed for such, are sometimes born without one; or perhaps it withers for want of exercise. However that may be, Dr. Blair has such a brain as Shakespeare somewhere describes as "dry as the remainder biscuit after a voyage."

I take it for granted that these good men are philosophically correct (for they are both agreed upon the subject) in their account of the origin of language; and if the Scripture had left us in the dark upon that article, I should very readily adopt their hypothesis for want of better information. I should suppose, for instance, that man made his first effort in speech in the way of an interjection, and that " Ah," or " Oh," being uttered with wonderful gesticulation, and variety of attitude, must have left his powers of expression quite exhausted; that in a course of time he would invent names for many things, but first for the objects of his daily wants. An apple would consequently be called an apple, and perhaps not many years would elapse before the appellation would receive the sanction of general use. In this case, and upon this supposition, seeing one in the hand of another man, he would exclaim, with a most moving pathos, " O apple!" Well and good,—" O apple!" is a very affecting speech, but in the mean time it profits him nothing. The man that holds it eats it, and *he* goes away with " O apple!" in his mouth, and with nothing better. Reflecting upon his disappointment, and that perhaps it arose from his not being more explicit, he contrives a term to denote his idea of transfer or gratuitous communication, and, the next occasion that offers of a similar kind, performs his part accordingly. His speech now stands thus, " Oh, give apple!" The apple-holder perceives himself called upon to part with his fruit, and having satisfied his own hunger, is perhaps not unwilling to do so. But unfortunately there is still room for a mistake; and a third person being present, he gives the apple to *him*.

Again disappointed, and again perceiving that his language has not all the precision that is requisite, the orator retires to his study, and there, after much deep thinking, conceives that the insertion of a pronoun, whose office shall be to signify that he not only wants the apple to be given, but given to himself, will remedy all defects, he uses it the next opportunity, and succeeds to a wonder, obtains the apple, and by his success such credit to his invention that pronouns continue to be in great repute ever after.

Now, as my two syllable-mongers, Beattie and Blair, both agree that language was originally inspired, and that the great variety of languages we find upon earth at present took its rise from the confusion of tongues at Babel, I am not perfectly convinced that there is any just occasion to invent this very ingenious solution of a difficulty which Scripture has solved already. My opinion however is, if I may presume to have an opinion of my own, so different from those who are so much wiser than myself, that if man had been his own teacher, and had acquired his words and his phrases only as necessity or convenience had prompted, his progress must have been considerably slower than it was, and in Homer's days the production of such a poem as the Iliad impossible. On the contrary, I doubt not that Adam on the very day of his creation was able to express himself in terms both forcible and elegant, and that he was at no loss for sublime diction and logical combination when he wanted to praise his Maker.

Yours, my dear friend.

XLII.

ENCLOSING THE MSS. OF "THE TASK."

To the Rev. William Unwin.

October 10, 1784.

My dear William, — I send you four quires of verse, which having sent, I shall dismiss from my thoughts and think no more of, till I see them in print.[1] I have not, after all, found time or industry enough to give the last hand to the points. I believe, however, they are not very erroneous, though in so long a work, and in a work that requires nicety in this particular, some inaccuracies will escape. Where you find any, you will oblige me by correcting them.

In some passages, especially in the second book, you will observe me very satirical. Writing on such subjects, I could not be otherwise. I can write nothing without aiming at least at usefulness: it were beneath my years to do it, and still more dishonorable to my religion. I know that a reformation of such abuses as I have censured is not to be expected from the efforts of a poet; but to contemplate the world, its follies, its vices, its indifference to duty, and its strenuous attachment to what is evil, and not to reprehend, were to approve it. From this charge at

---

[1] Lady Austen also had the honor of suggesting to Cowper the subject of this work, which made him the most popular poet of his age. "The Task" was begun early in the summer of 1783, but never mentioned to either Mr. Unwin or Mr. Newton until it was finished.

least I shall be clear, for I have neither tacitly nor expressly flattered either its characters or its customs. I have paid one, and only one compliment, which was so justly due that I did not know how to withhold it, especially having so fair an occasion, — I forget myself, there is another in the first book to Mr. Throckmorton, — but the compliment I mean is to Mr. Smith. It is however so managed that nobody but himself can make the application, and you, to whom I disclose the secret; a delicacy, on my part, which so much delicacy on his obliged me to the observance of.

What there is of a religious cast in the volume I have thrown towards the end of it, for two reasons: first, that I might not revolt the reader at his entrance; and secondly, that my best impressions might be made last. Were I to write as many volumes as Lope de Vega, or Voltaire, not one of them would be without this tincture. If the world like it not, so much the worse for them. I make all the concessions I can, that I may please them, but I will not please them at the expense of conscience.

My descriptions are all from Nature; not one of them second-handed. My delineations of the heart are from my own experience: not one of them borrowed from books, or in the least degree conjectural. In my numbers, which I have varied as much as I could (for blank verse without variety of numbers is no better than bladder and string), I have imitated nobody, though sometimes perhaps there may be an apparent resemblance; because at the same time that I would not imitate, I have not affectedly differed.

If the work cannot boast a regular plan (in which respect however I do not think it altogether indefensible), it may yet boast that the reflections are naturally suggested always by the preceding passage, and that except the fifth book, which is rather of a political aspect, the whole has one tendency, — to discountenance the modern enthusiasm after a London life, and to recommend rural ease and leisure as friendly to the cause of piety and virtue.

If it pleases you, I shall be happy, and collect from your pleasure in it an omen of its general acceptance.

Yours, my dear friend.

XLIII.

INTENTION OF COMPLETING POEM ON SCHOOL EDUCATION.

To the Rev. William Unwin.

October 20, 1784.

MY DEAR WILLIAM, — Your letter has relieved me from some anxiety, and given me a good deal of positive pleasure. I have faith in your judgment, and an implicit confidence in the sincerity of your approbation. The writing of so long a poem is a serious business; and the author must know little of his own heart who does not in some degree suspect himself of partiality to his own production; and who is he that would not be mortified by the discovery that he had written five thousand lines in vain? The poem however which you have in hand will not of itself make a volume so large as the last, or as a bookseller would wish. I say this because when I had sent Johnson five thousand verses, he applied for a thousand more. Two years since I began a piece [1] which grew to the length of two hundred, and there stopped. I have lately resumed it, and (I believe) shall finish it. But the subject is fruitful, and will not be comprised in a smaller compass than seven or eight hundred verses. It turns on the question whether an education at school or at home be preferable, and I shall give the preference to the latter. I mean that it shall pursue the track of the former, — that is to say, that it shall visit Stock in its way to publication. My design also is to inscribe it to you. But you must see it first; and if, after having seen it, you should have any objection, though it should be no bigger than the tittle of an *i*, I will deny myself that pleasure, and find no fault with your refusal. I have not been without thoughts of adding John Gilpin at the tail of all. He has made a good deal of noise in the world, and perhaps it may not be amiss to show that though I write generally with a serious intention, I know how to be occasionally merry. The Critical Reviewers charged me with an attempt at humor. John having been more celebrated upon the score of humor than most pieces that have appeared in modern days, may serve to exonerate me from the imputation; but in this article I am entirely under your judgment, and mean to be set down by it. All these together will make an octavo like the last. I should have told you that the piece which now employs me is in

---

[1] Tirocinium. See Poems.

rhyme. I do not intend to write any more blank. It is more difficult than rhyme, and not so amusing in the composition.[1] If, when you make the offer of my book to Johnson, he should stroke his chin, and look up to the ceiling, and cry " Humph!" anticipate him (I beseech you) at once, by saying "that you know I should be sorry that he should undertake for me to his own disadvantage, or that my volume should be in any degree pressed upon him. I make him the offer merely because I think he would have reason to complain of me, if I did not." But that punctilio once satisfied, it is a matter of indifference to me what publisher sends me forth. If Longman should have difficulties, which is the more probable, as I understand from you that he does not in these cases see with his own eyes, but will consult a brother poet, take no pains to conquer them. The idea of being hawked about, and especially of your being the hawker, is insupportable. Nichols (I have heard) is the most learned printer of the present day. He may be a man of taste as well as of learning; and I suppose that you would not want a gentleman usher to introduce you. He prints the Gentleman's Magazine, and may serve us, if the others should decline; if not, give yourself no farther trouble about the matter. I may possibly envy authors who can afford to publish at their own expense, and in that case should write no more. But the mortification would not break my heart.

. . . .

[1] He must have meant any original composition, since his translation of Homer into blank verse was already projected.

XLIV.

A MOTTO FOR "TIROCINIUM" WANTED.

To the Rev. William Bull.[1]

November 8, 1784.

My good Friend,— "The Task," as you know, is gone to the press; since it went I have been employed in writing another poem, which I am now transcribing, and which in a short time I design shall follow. It is intituled "Tirocinium, or a Review of Schools." The business and purpose of it are, to censure the want of discipline and the scandalous inattention to morals that obtain in them, especially in the largest; and to recommend private tuition as a mode of education preferable on all accounts; to call upon fathers to become tutors, of their own sons, where that is practicable; to take home a domestic tutor, where it is not; and if neither can be done, to place them under the care of such a man as he to whom I am writing,— some rural parson, whose attention is limited to a few.

Now what want I? A motto. I have taken mottoes from Virgil and Horace till I begin to fear lest the world should discover (what indeed is the

---

[1] A dissenting minister, settled in the adjacent town of Newport Pagnell, who had been introduced to Cowper by Mr. Newton shortly before his departure from Olney. Mr. Bull at first visited Cowper out of compassion; but the two men soon became attached on the basis of congenial tastes and cultivated minds, maintaining a close friendship always afterwards.

case) that I have no other authors of the Roman class. Find me one therefore in any of your multitudinous volumes, no matter whether it be taken from Burgersdicius, Bogtrottius, or Puddengulpius; the more recondite the better, — the world will suppose that at least I am familiar with the author whom I quote, and though the supposition will be an erroneous one, it will do them no harm, and me some good.

When you have found it, bring it with you, either to-morrow, Saturday, or Monday. One of those three days you and your son must dine with us. Choose, and let us know which you choose, in an answer by the bearer.

Yours, with our joint love to Mrs. Bull.

XLV.

ON THE DEATH OF MR. HILL'S MOTHER.

To Joseph Hill, Esq.

November, 1784.

My dear Friend, — To condole with you on the death of a mother aged eighty-seven would be absurd; rather therefore, as is reasonable, I congratulate you on the almost singular felicity of having enjoyed the company of so amiable and so near a relation so long. Your lot and mine in this respect have been very different, as, indeed, in almost every other. Your mother lived to see you rise, at least to see you comfortably established in the world; mine, dying when I was six years old, did not live to see me sink in it. You may remember with pleasure, while you live, a blessing vouchsafed to you so long; and I, while I live, must regret a comfort of which I was deprived so early. I can truly say that not a week passes (perhaps I might with equal veracity say a day) in which I do not think of her. Such was the impression her tenderness made upon me, though the opportunity she had for showing it was so short. But the ways of God are equal; and when I reflect on the pangs she would have suffered had she been a witness of all mine, I see more cause to rejoice than to mourn, that she was hidden in the grave so soon.

We have, as you say, lost a lively and sensible neighbor in Lady Austen; but we have been long accustomed to a state of retirement within one degree of solitude, and being naturally lovers of still life, can relapse into our former duality without being unhappy at the change. To me, indeed, a third is not necessary, while I can have the companion I have had these twenty years.

I am gone to the press again; a volume of mine will greet your hands some time either in the course of the winter or early in the spring. You will find it, perhaps, on the whole more entertaining than the former, as it treats a greater variety of subjects, and those, at least the most, of a sublunary kind. It will consist of a poem, in six books, called "The Task." To which will be added another, which I finished yesterday, called, I believe, "Tirocinium," on the subject of education.

You perceive that I have taken your advice, and given the pen no rest.

XLVI.

DEFENDING THE TITLE OF "THE TASK" AND OF ITS SEPARATE BOOKS

To the Rev. John Newton.

December 11, 1784.

MY DEAR FRIEND, — Having imitated no man, I may reasonably hope that I shall not incur the disadvantage of a comparison with my betters. Milton's manner was peculiar; so is Thomson's. He that should write like either of them would, in my judgment, deserve the name of a copyist, but not of a poet. A judicious and sensible reader therefore, like yourself, will not say that my manner is not good, because it does not resemble theirs, but will rather consider what it is in itself. Blank verse is susceptible of a much greater diversification of manner, than verse in rhyme; and why the modern writers of it have all thought proper to cast their numbers alike, I know not. Certainly it was not necessity that compelled them to it. I flatter myself, however, that I have avoided that sameness with others which would entitle me to nothing but a share in one common oblivion with them all. It is possible that, as the reviewer of my former volume found cause to say that he knew not to what class of writers to refer me, the reviewer of this, whosoever he shall be, may see occasion to remark the same singularity. At any rate, though as little apt to be sanguine as most men, and more prone to fear and despond, than to overrate my own productions, I am persuaded that I shall not forfeit anything by this volume that I gained by the last.

As to the title, I take it to be the best that is to be had. It is not possible that a book, including such a variety of subjects, and in which no particular one is predominant, should find a title adapted to them all. In such a case it seemed almost necessary to accommodate the name to the incident that gave birth to the poem;[1] nor does it appear to me that because I performed more than my task, therefore the Task is not a suitable title. A house would still be a house, though the builder of it should make it ten times as big as he at first intended. I might indeed, following the example of the Sunday newsmonger, call it the Olio. But I should do myself wrong; for though it have much variety, it has, I trust, no confusion.

For the same reason none of the interior titles apply themselves to the contents at large of that book to which they belong. They are, every one of them, taken either from the leading (I should say the introductory) passage of that particular book, or from that which makes the most conspicuous figure in it. Had I set off with a design to write upon a gridiron, and had I actually written near two hundred lines upon that utensil, as I have upon the Sofa, the Gridiron should have been my title. But the Sofa being,

[1] Lady Austen had often urged him to try his powers in blank verse; at last he promised to comply with her request, if she would give him a subject. "Oh," she replied, "you can never be in want of a subject; you can write upon any; — write upon this Sofa!"

as I may say, the starting-post from which I addressed myself to the long race that I soon conceived a design to run, it acquired a just pre-eminence in my account, and was very worthily advanced to the titular honor it enjoys, its right being at least so far a good one, that no word in the language could pretend a better.

The Time-piece appears to me (though by some accident the import of that title has escaped you) to have a degree of propriety beyond the most of them. The book to which it belongs is intended to strike the hour that gives notice of approaching judgment, and dealing pretty largely in the *signs* of the *times*, seems to be denominated, as it is, with a sufficient degree of accommodation to the subject.

As to the word *worm*, it is the very appellation which Milton himself, in a certain passage of the Paradise Lost, gives to the serpent. Not having the book at hand, I cannot now refer to it; but I am sure of the fact. I am mistaken, too, if Shakespeare's Cleopatra do not call the asp, by which she thought fit to destroy herself, by the same name. But not having read the play these five-and-twenty years, I will not affirm it. They are, however, without all doubt, convertible terms. A worm is a small serpent, and a serpent is a large worm. And when an epithet significant of the most terrible species of those creatures is adjoined, the idea is surely sufficiently ascertained. No animal of the vermicular or serpentine kind is crested, but the most formidable of all.

We do not often see, or rather feel, so severe a frost before Christmas. Unexpected at least by me, it had like to have been too much for my greenhouse, my myrtles having found themselves yesterday morning in an atmosphere so cold that the mercury was fallen eight degrees below the freezing-point.

We are truly sorry for Mrs. Newton's indisposition, and shall be glad to hear of her recovery. We are most liable to colds at this season, and at this season a cold is most difficult to cure.

Be pleased to remember us to the young ladies, and to all under your roof and elsewhere who are mindful of us, and believe me
Your affectionate.

Your letters are gone to their address. The oysters were very good.

XLVII.

JOHN GILPIN.—VANITY OF POPULAR APPLAUSE.

To the Rev. John Newton.

April 22, 1785.

MY DEAR FRIEND,— When I received your account of the great celebrity of John Gilpin, I felt myself both flattered and grieved. Being man, and having in my composition all the ingredients of which other men are made, and vanity among the rest, it pleased me to reflect that I was on a sudden become so famous, and that all the world was busy inquiring after me; but the next moment, recollecting my former self, and that thirteen years ago, as harmless as John's history is, I should not then have written it, my spirits sank, and I was ashamed of my success.

Your letter was followed the next post by one from Mr. Unwin. You tell me that I am rivalled by Mrs. Bellamy;[1] and he, that I have a competitor for fame, not less formidable, in the Learned Pig. Alas! what is an author's popularity worth in a world that can suffer a prostitute on one side and a pig on the other to eclipse his brightest glories? I am therefore sufficiently humbled by these considerations; and unless I should hereafter be ordained to engross the public attention by means more magnificent than a song, am persuaded that I shall suffer no real detriment by their applause. I have produced many things under the influence of despair which hope would not have permitted to spring. But if the soil of that melancholy in which I have walked so long has thrown up here and there an unprofitable fungus, it is well, at least, that it is not chargeable with having brought forth poison. Like you, I see, or think I can see, that Gilpin may have his use. Causes, in appearance trivial, produce often the most beneficial consequences; and perhaps my volumes may now travel to a distance which, if they had not been ushered into the world by that notable horseman, they would never have reached.

I hope that neither the master of St. Paul's nor any other school, who may have commenced my admirer on John's account, will write to me for such a reason; yet a little while, and if they have laughed with me, their note will be changed, and perhaps they will revile me. "Tirocinium" is no friend of theirs; on the

---

[1] A celebrated actress, who wrote her memoirs, which were much read at that time.

contrary, if it have the effect I wish it to have, it will prove much their enemy, for it gives no quarter to modern pedagogues, but finding them all alike guilty of supineness and neglect in the affair of morals, condemns them, both schoolmasters and heads of colleges, without distinction. Our temper differs somewhat from that of the ancient Jews. They would neither dance nor weep. We indeed weep not if a man mourn unto us; but I must needs say that if he pipe we seem disposed to dance with the greatest alacrity. I ought to tell you that this remark has a reference to John Gilpin; otherwise, having been jumbled a little out of its place, you might be at a loss for the explication.

Yours.

XLVIII.

REWARDS OF FAME.

To the Rev. William Unwin.

April 30, 1785.

MY DEAR FRIEND, — I return you thanks for a letter so warm with the intelligence of the celebrity of John Gilpin. I little thought, when I mounted him upon my Pegasus, that he would become so famous. I have learned also, from Mr. Newton, that he is equally renowned in Scotland, and that a lady there had undertaken to write a second part, on the subject of Mrs. Gilpin's return to London, but not succeeding in it as she wished, she dropped it. He tells me, likewise, that the head master of St.

Paul's school (who he is I know not) has conceived, in consequence of the entertainment that John has afforded him, a vehement desire to write to me. Let us hope he will alter his mind; for should we even exchange civilities upon the occasion, " Tirocinium" will spoil all. The great estimation, however, in which this knight of the stone-bottles is held may turn out a circumstance propitious to the volume of which his history will make a part. Those events that prove the prelude to our greatest success are often apparently trivial in themselves, and such as seemed to promise nothing. The disappointment that Horace mentions is reversed, — We design a mug, and it proves a hogshead. It is a little hard that I alone should be unfurnished with a printed copy of this facetious story. When you visit London next, you must buy the most elegant impression of it and bring it with you. I thank you also for writing to Johnson. I likewise wrote to him myself. Your letter and mine together have operated to admiration. There needs nothing more but that the effect be lasting, and the whole will soon be printed. We now draw towards the middle of the fifth book of "The Task." The man, Johnson, is like unto some vicious horses that I have known. They would not budge till they were spurred, and when they were spurred they would kick. So did he. His temper was somewhat disconcerted; but his pace was quickened, and I was contented.

I was very much pleased with the following sentence in Mr. Newton's last: " I am perfectly satisfied with the propriety of your proceeding as to the publication." Now, therefore, we are friends again. Now he once more inquires after the work which, till he had disburthened himself of this acknowledgment, neither he nor I in any of our letters to each other ever mentioned. Some side-wind has wafted to him a report of those reasons by which I justified my conduct.[1] I never made a secret of them, but both your mother and I have studiously deposited them with those who we thought were most likely to transmit them to him. They wanted only a hearing, which once obtained, their solidity and cogency were such that they were sure to prevail.

You mention Bensley. I formerly knew the man you mention, but his elder brother much better. We were schoolfellows, and he was one of a club of seven Westminster men, to which I belonged, who dined together every Thursday. Should it please God to give me ability to perform the poet's part to some purpose, many whom I once called friends, but who have since treated me with a most magnificent indifference, will be ready to take me by the hand again, and some, whom I never held in that estimation, will, like Bensley (who was but a boy when I left London), boast of a connection with me which they never had. Had I the virtues and graces and accomplishments of Saint Paul himself, I might have them at Olney and nobody would care a button about me, yourself and one or two more excepted. Fame begets favor; and one talent, if it be rubbed a little bright by use

---

[1] An allusion to Cowper's failure to confide in Newton while writing "The Task," — a circumstance which had caused some coolness on Newton's part.

and practice, will procure a man more friends than a thousand virtues. Dr. Johnson, I remember, in the life of one of our poets (I believe of Savage), says that he retired from the world, flattering himself that he should be regretted. But the world never missed him. I think his observation upon it is that the vacancy made by the retreat of any individual is soon filled up; that a man may always be obscure if he chooses to be so, and that he who neglects the world will be by the world neglected.

Your mother and I walked yesterday in the Wilderness. As we entered the gate, a glimpse of something white contained in a little hole in the gate-post caught my eye. I looked again, and discovered a bird's nest with two tiny eggs in it. By and by they will be fledged and tailed, and get wing-feathers, and fly. My case is somewhat similar to that of the parent bird. My nest is in a little nook. Here I brood and hatch, and in due time my progeny takes wing and whistles.

We wait for the time of your coming with pleasant expectation.

Yours truly.

XLIX.

HIS OWN STATE OF MIND AND PROVIDENTIAL CONNECTION WITH MR. NEWTON.

To the Rev. John Newton.

May, 1785.

MY DEAR FRIEND, — ... I am sensible of the tenderness and affectionate kindness with which you recollect our past intercourse, and express your hopes of my future restoration. I, too, within the last eight months have had my hopes, though they have been of short duration, cut off like the foam upon the waters. Some previous adjustments, indeed, are necessary, before a lasting expectation of comfort can take place in me. There are those persuasions in my mind which either entirely forbid the entrance of hope, or, if it enter, immediately eject it. They are incompatible with any such inmate, and must be turned out themselves before so desirable a guest can possibly have secured possession. This, you say, will be done. It may be, but it is not done yet; nor has a single step in the course of God's dealings with me been taken towards it. If I mend, no creature ever mended so slowly that recovered at last. I am like a slug or snail, that has fallen into a deep well; slug as he is, he performs his descent with an alacrity proportioned to his weight; but he does not crawl up again quite so fast. Mine was a rapid plunge; but my return to daylight, if I am indeed returning, is leisurely enough. — I wish you a swift progress, and a pleasant one, through the great subject that you have in hand; and set that value upon your letters to which they are in themselves entitled, but which is certainly increased by that peculiar attention which the writer of them pays to me. Were I such as I once was, I should say that I have a claim upon your particular notice which nothing ought to supersede. Most of your other connections you may fairly be said to have formed by your own act; but your connection with me was the work of God. The kine that went up with the ark from Bethshemesh left what they loved behind them, in obedience to an impression which to them was perfectly dark and unintelligible. Your journey to Huntingdon was not less wonderful. He indeed, who sent you, knew well wherefore, but you knew not. That dispensation therefore would furnish me, as long as we can both remember it, with a plea for some distinction at your hands, had I occasion to use and urge it, which I have not. But I am altered since that time; and if your affection for me had ceased, you might very reasonably justify your change by mine. I can say nothing for myself at present; but this I can venture to foretell, that should the restoration of which my friends assure me obtain, I shall undoubtedly love those who have continued to love me, even in a state of transformation from my former self, much more than ever. I doubt not that Nebuchadnezzar had friends in his prosperity; all kings have many. But when his nails became like eagles' claws, and he ate grass like an ox, I suppose he had few to pity him.

. . . . . .

I am glad that Johnson is in fact a civiller man than I supposed him. My quarrel with him was not for any stricture of his upon my poetry (for he has made several, and many of them have been judicious, and my work will be the better for them), but for a certain rudeness with which he questioned my judgment of a writer of the last century, though I only mention the effect that his verses had upon me when a boy. There certainly was at the time a bustle in his temper, occasioned, I imagine, by my being a little importunate with him to proceed. He has however recovered himself since; and except that the press seems to have stood still this last week, has printed as fast as I could wish. Had he kept the same pace from the beginning, the book had been published, as indeed it ought to have been, three months ago. That evil report of his indolence reaches me from everybody that knows him, and is so general that had I a work or the publication of one in hand, the expenses of which I intended to take the hazard of upon myself, I should be very much afraid to employ him. He who will neglect himself cannot well be expected to attend to the interests of another.

— L.

DESCRIPTION OF HIS SUMMER-HOUSE.

To Joseph Hill, Esq.

June 25, 1785.

MY DEAR FRIEND, — I write in a nook that I call my Boudoir. It is a summer-house not much bigger than a sedan chair, the door of which opens into the garden, that is now crowded with pinks, roses, and honeysuckles, and the window into my neighbor's orchard. It formerly served an apothecary, now dead, as a smoking-room; and under my feet is a trap-door, which once covered a hole in the ground, where he kept his bottles. At present, however, it is dedicated to sublimer uses. Having lined it with garden mats, and furnished it with a table and two chairs, here I write all that I write in summertime, whether to my friends or to the public. It is secure from all noise, and refuge from all intrusion; for intruders sometimes trouble me in the winter evenings at Olney. But (thanks to my Boudoir!) I can now hide myself from them. A poet's retreat is sacred. They acknowledge the truth of that proposition, and never presume to violate it.

The last sentence puts me in mind to tell you that I have ordered my volume to your door. My bookseller is the most dilatory of all his fraternity, or you would have received it long since. It is more than a month since I returned him the last proof, and consequently since the printing was finished. I sent him the manuscript at the beginning of last November, that he might publish while the town was full; — and he will hit the exact moment when it is entirely empty. Patience (you will perceive) is in no situation exempted from the severest trials; a remark that may serve to comfort you under the numberless trials of your own.

LI.

FAVORABLE RECEPTION OF HIS VOLUME BY THE PUBLIC. — NEGLECT OF HIS OLD FRIENDS.

To the Rev. John Newton.

July 9, 1785.

MY DEAR FRIEND, — You wrong your own judgment when you represent it as not to be trusted; and mine, if you suppose that I have that opinion of it. Had you disapproved, I should have been hurt and mortified. No man's disapprobation would have hurt me more. Your favorable sentiments of my book must consequently give me pleasure in the same proportion. By the post, last Sunday, I had a letter from Lord Dartmouth, in which he thanked me for my volume, of which he had read only a part. Of that part, however, he expresses himself in terms with which my authorship has abundant cause to be satisfied; and adds that the specimen has made him impatient for the whole. I have likewise received a letter from a judicious friend of mine in London, and a man of fine taste, unknown to you, who speaks of it in the same language. Fortified by these cordials, I feel myself qualified to face the world without much anxiety, and delivered in a great measure from those fears which I suppose all men feel upon the like occasion.

My first volume I sent, as you may remember, to the Lord Chancellor, accompanied by a friendly but respectful epistle. His Lordship, however, thought it not worth his while to return me any answer, or to take the least notice of my present. I sent it also to Colman, manager of the Haymarket Theatre, with whom I once was intimate. He likewise proved too great a man to recollect me; and though he has published since, did not account it necessary to return the compliment. I have allowed myself to be a little pleased with an opportunity to show them that I resent their treatment of me, and have sent this book to neither of them. They, indeed, are the former friends to whom I particularly allude in my epistle to Mr. Hill; and it is possible that they may take to themselves a censure that they so well deserve. If not, it matters not; for I shall never have any communication with them hereafter.

If Mr. Bates has found it difficult to furnish you with a motto to your volumes, I have no reason to imagine that I shall do it easily. I shall not leave my books unransacked; but there is something so new and peculiar in the occasion that suggested your subject, that I question whether, in all the classics, can be found a sentence suited to it. Our sins and follies, in this country, assume a shape that Heathen writers had never any opportunity to notice. They deified the dead, indeed, but not in the Temple of Jupiter. The new-made god had an altar of his own; and they conducted the ceremony without sacrilege or confusion. It is possible, however, and I think barely so, that somewhat may occur susceptible of accommodation to your purpose; and if it should, I shall be happy to serve you with it.

I told you, I believe, that the Spinney has been cut down; and though it may seem sufficient to have mentioned such an occurrence once, I cannot help recurring to the melancholy theme. Last night, at near nine o'clock, we entered it for the first time this summer. We had not walked many yards in it, before we perceived that this pleasant retreat is destined never to be a pleasant retreat again. In one more year the whole will be a thicket. That which was once the serpentine walk is now in a state of transformation, and is already become as woody as the rest. Poplars and elms without number are springing in the turf. They are now as high as the knee. Before the summer is ended, they will be twice as high; and the growth of another season will make them trees. It will then be impossible for any but a sportsman and his dog to penetrate it. The desolation of the whole scene is such that it sunk our spirits. The ponds are dry. The circular one in front of the hermitage is filled with flags and rushes; so that, if it contains any water, not a drop is visible. The weeping-willow at the side of it, the only ornamental plant that has escaped the axe, is dead. The ivy and the moss, with which the hermitage was lined, are torn away; and the very mats that covered the benches have been stripped off, rent in tatters, and trodden under foot. So farewell, Spinney; I have promised myself that I will never enter it again. We have both prayed in it, — you for me, and I for you. But it is desecrated from this time forth, and the voice of prayer will be heard in it no more. The fate of it in this respect, however deplorable, is not peculiar. The spot where Jacob anointed his pillar, and (which is more apposite) the spot once honored with the presence of Him who dwelt in the bush, have long since suffered similar disgrace, and are become common ground.

There is great severity in the application of the text you mention, — I am *their music*. But it is not the worse for that. We both approve it highly. The other in Ezekiel does not seem quite so pat. The prophet complains that his word was to the people like a pleasant song, heard with delight but soon forgotten. At the commemoration[1] I suppose that the word is nothing, but the music all in all. The Bible, however, will abundantly supply you with applicable passages. All passages, indeed, that animadvert upon the profanation of God's house and worship, seem to present themselves upon the occasion.

We have returned thanks to Mr. Wm. Unwin for a turbot and lobster, and he disclaims all right to the acknowledgment. Is it due to you and Mrs. Newton? If it be, accept a grateful one, accept likewise our love and best wishes; and believe me, my dear friend, with warm and true affection,

     Yours.

LII.

SELF-ABASEMENT. — "THE TASK" NOT ADVERTISED.

To the Rev. John Newton.

August 6, 1785.

My dear Friend, — I found your account of what you experienced in your state of maiden authorship very entertaining because very natural. I suppose that no man ever made his first sally from the press without a conviction that all eyes and ears would be engaged to attend him; at least, without a thousand anxieties lest they should not. But, however arduous and interesting such an enterprise may be in the first instance, it seems to me that our feelings on the occasion soon become obtuse. I can answer, at 'least, for

[1] Commemoration of Handel in Westminster Abbey.

one. Mine are by no means what they were when I published my first volume. I am even so indifferent to the matter that I can truly assert myself guiltless of the very idea of my book sometimes whole days together. God knows that, my mind having been occupied more than twelve years in the contemplation of the most tremendous subjects, the world and its opinion of what I write is become as unimportant to me as the whistling of a bird in a bush. Despair made amusement necessary, and I found poetry the most agreeable amusement. Had I not endeavored to perform my best, it would not have amused me at all. The mere blotting of so much paper would have been but indifferent sport. God gave me grace also to wish that I might not write in vain. Accordingly, I have mingled much truth with much trifle, and such truths as deserved, at least, to be clad as well and as handsomely as I could clothe them. If the world approve me not, so much the worse for them, but not for me. I have only endeavored to serve them, and the loss will be their own. And as to their commendations, if I should chance to win them, I feel myself equally invulnerable there. The view that I have had of myself for many years has been so truly humiliating that I think the praises of all mankind could not hurt me. God knows that I speak my present sense of the matter, at least most truly, when I say that the admiration of creatures like myself seems to me a weapon the least dangerous that my worst enemy could employ against me. I am fortified against it by such solidity of real self-abasement, that I deceive myself most egregiously if I do not heartily despise it. Praise belongeth to God; and I seem to myself to covet it no more than I covet divine honors. Could I assuredly hope that God would at last deliver me, I should have reason to thank him for all that I have suffered, were it only for the sake of this single fruit of my affliction, — that it has taught me how much more contemptible I am in myself than I ever before suspected, and has reduced my former share of self-knowledge (of which at that time I had a tolerable good opinion) to a mere nullity, in comparison with what I have acquired since. Self is a subject of inscrutable misery and mischief, and can never be studied to so much advantage as in the dark; for as the bright beams of the sun seem to impart a beauty to the foulest objects, and can make even a dunghill smile, so the light of God's countenance, vouchsafed to a fallen creature, so sweetens him and softens him for the time, that he seems, both to others and to himself, to have nothing savage or sordid about him. But the heart is a nest of serpents, and will be such while it continues to beat. If God cover the mouth of that nest with his hand, they are hushed and snug; but if he withdraw his hand, the whole family lift up their heads and hiss, and are as active and venomous as ever. This I always professed to believe from the time that I had embraced the truth, but never knew it as I know it now. To what end I have been made to know it as I do, whether for the benefit of others or for my own, or for both, or for neither, will appear hereafter.

What I have written leads me naturally to the mention of a matter that I had forgot. I should blame nobody, not even my intimate friends, and those who have the most favorable opinion of me, were they to charge the publication of " John Gilpin," at the end of so much solemn and serious truth, to the score of the author's vanity; and to suspect that, however sober I may be upon proper occasions, I have yet that itch for popularity that would not suffer me to sink my title to a jest that had been so successful. But the case is not such. When I sent the copy of " The Task " to Johnson, I desired, indeed, Mr. Unwin to ask him the question, whether or not he would choose to make it a part of the volume? This I did merely with a view to promote the sale of it. Johnson answered, " By all means." Some months afterward, he enclosed a note to me in one of my packets, in which he expressed a change of mind, alleging that to print " John Gilpin " would only be to print what had been hackneyed in every magazine, in every shop, and at the corner of every street. I answered, that I desired to be entirely governed by his opinion; and that if he chose to waive it, I should be better pleased with the omission. Nothing more passed between us upon the subject, and I concluded that I should never have the immortal honor of being generally known as the author of " John Gilpin." In the last packet, however, down came John, very fairly printed, and equipped for public appearance. The business having taken this turn, I concluded that Johnson had adopted my original thought, that it might prove advantageous to the sale; and as he had had the trouble and expense of printing it, I corrected the copy and let it pass. Perhaps, however, neither the book nor the writer may be made much more famous by John's good company, than they would have been without it; for the volume has never yet been advertised, nor can I learn that Johnson intends it. He fears the expense, and the consequence must be prejudicial. Many who would purchase will remain uninformed; but I am perfectly content.

My compliment to Mr. Throckmorton was printed before he had cut down the Spinney. He indeed has not cut it down, but Mr. Morley, the tenant, — with the owner's consent, however, no doubt. My poetical civilities, however, were due to that gentleman for more solid advantages conferred upon me in prose; without any solicitation on our part, or even a hint that we wished it (it was indeed a favor that we could not have aspired to), he made us a present of a key of his kitchen garden, and of the fruit of it whenever we pleased. That key, I believe, was never given to any other person; nor is it likely that they should give it to many, for it is their favorite walk, and was the only one in which they could be secure from all interruption. They seem, however, to have left the country, and it is possible that he may never know that my Muse has noticed him.

I have considered your motto, and like the purport of it; but the best, because the most laconic manner of it seems to be this, —

Cum talis sis, sis noster;

utinam being, in my account of it, unnecessary.

Mrs. Newton has our hearty thanks for the turbot and lobster, which were excellent. To her and to the young ladies we beg to be affectionately remembered.

Three weeks since, Mr. Unwin and his late ward, Miss Shuttleworth, and John, called on us in their way from the north, having made an excursion so far as to Dumfries. Mr. Unwin desired me to say that though he had been often in town since he had the pleasure of seeing you last, he had always gone thither on business, and making a short stay, had not been able to find an opportunity to pay his respects to you again.

Yours, my dear friend, most truly.

LIII.

REASONS FOR PUBLISHING "THE EPISTLE TO JOSEPH HILL."

To Joseph Hill, Esq.

October 11, 1785.

MY DEAR SIR, — You began your letter with an apology for long silence, and it is now incumbent upon me to do the same; and the rather, as your kind invitation to Wargrave entitled you to a speedier answer. The truth is, that I am become, if not a man of business, yet a busy man, and have been engaged almost this twelvemonth in a work that will allow of no long interruption. On this account it was impossible for me to accept your obliging summons; and having only to tell you that I could not, it appeared to me as a matter of no great moment, whether you received that intelligence soon or late.

You do me justice when you ascribe my printed epistle to you, to my friendship for you; though, in fact, it was equally owing to the opinion that I have of yours for me. Having, in one part or other of my two volumes, distinguished by name the majority of those few for whom I entertain a friendship, it seemed to me that it would be unjustifiable negligence to omit yourself; and if I took that step without communicating to you my intention, it was only to gratify myself the more, with the hope of surprising you agreeably. Poets are dangerous persons to be acquainted with, especially if a man have that in his character that promises to shine in verse. To that very circumstance it is owing, that you are now figuring away in mine. For notwithstanding what you say on the subject of honesty and friendship, that they are not splendid enough for public celebration, I must still think of them as I did before, — that there are no qualities of the mind and heart that can deserve it better. I can, at least for my own part, look round about upon the generality, and while I see them deficient in those grand requisites of a respectable character, am not able to discover that they possess any other, of value enough to atone for the want of them.

I beg that you will present my respects to Mrs. Hill, and believe me
    Ever affectionately yours.

LIV.

REVIVAL OF AN OLD FRIENDSHIP.

To Lady Hesketh.[1]

October 12, 1785.

MY DEAR COUSIN, — It is no new thing with you to give pleasure; but I will venture to say that you do not often give more than you gave me this morning. When I came down to breakfast, and found upon the table a letter franked by my uncle,[2] and when opening that frank I found that it contained a letter from you, I said within myself, "This is just as it should be. We are all grown young again, and the days that I thought I should see no more are actually returned." You perceive, therefore, that you judged well when you conjectured that a line from you would not be disagreeable to me. It could not be otherwise than, as in fact it proved, a most agreeable surprise, for I can truly boast of an affection for you that neither years nor interrupted intercourse have at all abated. I need only recollect how much I valued you once, and with how much cause, immediately to

---

[1] Correspondence with Lady Hesketh had now been discontinued for eighteen years, Cowper's last letter to her (January 30, 1767) having been written in a strain of melancholy pietism in which she thought it dangerous for him to indulge. Now that she saw, by "John Gilpin" and "The Task," that he could once more indulge in the playful temper of his earlier years, she wrote to him in a way that showed that many years of absence and broken intercourse had made no change in her feelings towards him.

[2] Ashley Cowper, Lady Hesketh's father.

feel a revival of the same value; if that can be said to revive, which at the most has only been dormant for want of employment, but I slander it when I say that it has slept. A thousand times have I recollected a thousand scenes, in which our two selves have formed the whole of the drama with the greatest pleasure; at times, too, when I had no reason to suppose that I should ever hear from you again. I have laughed with you at the Arabian Nights Entertainment, which afforded us, as you well know, a fund of merriment that deserves never to be forgot. I have walked with you to Netley Abbey, and have scrambled with you over hedges in every direction, and many other feats we have performed together, upon the field of my remembrance, and all within these few years. Should I say within this twelvemonth, I should not transgress the truth. The hours that I have spent with you were among the pleasantest of my former days, and are therefore chronicled in my mind so deeply as to feel no erasure. Neither do I forget my poor friend, Sir Thomas. I should remember him indeed, at any rate, on account of his personal kindness to myself; but the last testimony that he gave of his regard for you endears him to me still more. With his uncommon understanding (for with many peculiarities he had more sense than any of his acquaintance) and with his generous sensibilities, it was hardly possible that he should not distinguish you as he has done. As it was the last, so it was the best proof that he could give, of a judgment that never deceived him, when he would allow himself leisure to consult it.

You say that you have often heard of me: that puzzles me. I cannot imagine from what quarter, but it is no matter. I must tell you, however, my cousin, that your information has been a little defective. That I am happy in my situation is true; I live, and have lived these twenty years, with Mrs. Unwin, to whose affectionate care of me during the far greater part of that time it is, under Providence, owing that I live at all. But I do not account myself happy in having been for thirteen of those years in a state of mind that has made all that care and attention necessary; an attention and a care that have injured her health, and which, had she not been uncommonly supported, must have brought her to the grave. But I will pass to another subject; it would be cruel to particularize only to give pain, neither would I by any means give a sable hue to the first letter of a correspondence so unexpectedly renewed.

I am delighted with what you tell me of my uncle's good health. To enjoy any measure of cheerfulness at so late a day is much; but to have that late day enlivened with the vivacity of youth is much more, and in these postdiluvian times a rarity indeed. Happy, for the most part, are parents who have daughters. Daughters are not apt to outlive their natural affections, which a son has generally survived, even before his boyish years are expired. I rejoice particularly in my uncle's felicity, who has three female descendants from his little person, who leave him nothing to wish for upon that head.

My dear cousin, dejection of spirits, which I suppose may have prevented many a man from becoming an author, made me one. I find constant employment necessary, and therefore take care to be constantly employed. Manual occupations do not engage the mind sufficiently, as I know by experience, having tried many. But composition, especially of verse, absorbs it wholly. I write therefore, generally, three hours in a morning, and in an evening I transcribe. I read also, but less than I write, for I must have bodily exercise, and therefore never pass a day without it.

You ask me where I have been this summer. I answer, at Olney. Should you ask me where I spent the last seventeen summers, I should still answer, at Olney. Ay, and the winters also: I have seldom left it, and except when I attended my brother in his last illness, never, I believe, a fortnight together.

Adieu, my beloved cousin. I shall not always be thus nimble in reply, but shall always have great pleasure in answering you when I can.

Yours, my dear friend and cousin.

LV.

CONCERNING MONEY AND FRIENDSHIP.

To Lady Hesketh.

OLNEY, *November* 9, 1785.

MY DEAREST COUSIN, — Whose last most affectionate letter has run in my head ever since I received it, and which I now sit down to answer two days sooner than the post will serve me; I thank you for it, and with a warmth for which I am sure you will give me credit, though I do not spend many words in describing it. I do not seek *new* friends, not being altogether sure that I should find them, but have unspeakable pleasure in being still beloved by an old one. I hope that now our correspondence has suffered its last interruption, and that we shall go down together to the grave, chatting and chirping as merrily as such a scene of things as this will permit.

I am happy that my poems have pleased you. My volume has afforded me no such pleasure at any time, either while I was writing it or since its publication, as I have derived from yours and my uncle's opinion of it. I make certain allowances for partiality, and for that peculiar quickness of taste with which you both relish what you like, and after all drawbacks upon those accounts duly made, find myself rich in the measure of your approbation that still remains. But above all, I honor John Gilpin, since it was he who first encouraged you to write. I made him on purpose to laugh at, and he served his purpose well; but I am now in debt to him for a more valuable acquisition than all the laughter in the world amounts to, — the recovery of my intercourse with you, which is to me inestimable. My benevolent and generous cousin, when I was once asked if I wanted anything, and given delicately to understand that the inquirer was ready to supply all my occasions, I thankfully and civilly, but positively, declined the favor. I neither suffer, nor have suffered, any such inconveniences as I had not much rather endure than come under obligations of that sort to a person comparatively with yourself a stranger to me. But to you I answer otherwise. I know you thoroughly, and the liberality of your disposition, and have that consummate confidence in the sincerity of your wish to serve me that delivers me from all awkward constraint, and from all fear of trespassing by acceptance. To you, therefore, I reply, Yes. Whensoever, and whatsoever, and in what manner-soever you please; and add moreover, that my affection for the giver is such as will increase to me tenfold the satisfaction that I shall have in receiving. It is necessary, however, that I should let you a little into the state of my finances, that you may not suppose them more narrowly circumscribed than they are. Since Mrs. Unwin and I have lived at Olney, we have had but one purse, although during the whole of that time, till lately, her income was nearly double mine. Her revenues indeed are now in some measure reduced, and do not much exceed my own; the worst consequence of this is that we are forced to deny ourselves some things which hitherto we have been better able to afford; but they are such things as neither life, nor the well-being of life, depend upon. My own income has been better than it is; but when it was best, it would not have enabled me to live as my connections demanded that I should, had it not been combined with a better than itself, at least at this end of the kingdom. Of this I had full proof during three months that I spent in lodgings at Huntingdon, in which time, by the help of good management and a clear notion of economical matters, I contrived to spend the income of a twelvemonth. Now, my beloved cousin, you are in possession of the whole case as it stands. Strain no points to your own inconvenience, or hurt, for there is no need of it, but indulge yourself in communicating (no matter what) that you can spare without missing it, since by so doing you will be sure to add to the comforts of my life one of the sweetest that I can enjoy, — a token and proof of your affection.

I cannot believe but that I should know you, notwithstanding all that time may have done: there is not a feature of your face, could I meet it upon the road, by itself, that I should not instantly recollect. I should say, that is my cousin's nose, or those are her lips and her chin, and no woman upon earth can claim them but herself. As for me, I am a very smart youth of my years; I am not indeed grown gray so much as I am grown bald. No matter; there was more hair in the world than ever had the honor to belong to me; accordingly, having found just enough to curl a little at my ears, and to intermix with a little of my own, that still hangs behind, I appear, if you see me in an afternoon, to have a very decent headdress, not easily distinguished from my natural growth, which, being worn with a small bag, and a black ribbon about my neck, continues to me the charms of my youth even on the verge of age. Away with the fear of writing too often!

P. S. That the view I give you of myself may be complete, I add the two following items: That I am in debt to nobody, and that I grow fat.

LVI.

LADY HESKETH'S BOUNTY. — TRANSLATION OF HOMER NO LONGER A SECRET.

To Lady Hesketh.

My dearest Cousin, — I am glad that I always loved you as I did. It releases me from any occasion to suspect that my present affection for you is indebted for its existence to any selfish considerations. No, I am sure I love you disinterestedly and for your own sake, because I never thought of you with any other sensations than those of the truest affection, even while I was under the influence of a persuasion that I should never hear from you again. But with my present feelings, superadded to those that I always had for you, I find it no easy matter to do justice to my sensations. I perceive myself in a state of mind similar to that of the traveller described in Pope's Messiah, who, as he passes through a sandy desert, starts at the sudden and unexpected sound of a waterfall. You have placed me in a situation new to me, and in which I feel myself somewhat puzzled how I ought to behave. At the same time that I would not grieve you by putting a check upon your bounty, I would be as careful not to abuse it as if I were a miser, and the question not about your money but my own.

Although I do not suspect that a secret to you, my cousin, is any burden, yet having maturely considered that point since I wrote my last, I feel myself altogether disposed to release you from the injunction to that effect under which I laid you. I have now made such a progress in my translation that I need neither fear that I shall stop short of the end, nor that any rider of Pegasus should overtake me. Therefore, if at any time it should fall fairly in your way, or you should feel yourself invited to say I am so occupied, you have my poetship's free permission. Dr. Johnson read and recommended my first volume.

LVII.

HAPPINESS IN THE RENEWAL OF AN OLD FRIENDSHIP. — POLITICS. — ON THE KING'S STAG-HUNTS.

To Lady Hesketh.

OLNEY, *November* 23, 1785.

MY DEAR COUSIN, — I am obliged to you for having allotted your morning to me, and not less obliged to you for writing, when the opportunity you had set apart for that purpose had been almost entirely consumed by others. It cost me some little deliberation to decide whether I should answer by this night's post, or whether I should wait till I could tell you that the wine is arrived; but to say the truth, I had it not in my power to wait; so I cut the matter short at once by determining to believe that the frequency of my letters will not make them a burden to you. I did not know or suspect that Providence had so much good in store for me in the present life as I promise myself now from the renewal of our intimacy. But it seems that my calculations upon that subject were erroneous ; it is renewed ; and I look forward to the permanence of it with the pleasantest expectations, and resolve to do all I can to deserve your punctual correspondence, by being as punctual as possible myself. *How easily are resolutions made and kept, when the whole heart is in them!*

Fifty things present themselves to me that I want to say ; and while each pleads for the preference, they all together so distract my choice that I hardly know with which to begin.

I thank you, my dearest cousin, for your medical advice. I have tried other wines, but never could meet with any that I could drink constantly, but port, without being the worse for it. And with respect to the quantity, that is a point that habit so effectually decides that after many years' practice, a limitation to a certain stint becomes in a manner necessary. When I have drunk what I always drink, I can feel that more would disgust me. I have, indeed, a most troublesome stomach, and which does not improve as I grow older. I have eaten nothing for some time past that it has not quarrelled with, from my bread and butter in the morning down to the egg that I generally make my supper. It constrains me to deny myself some things that I am fond of, and some that are in a degree necessary to health, or that seem to be so. Green tea I have not touched these twenty years, or only to be poisoned by it ; but bohea, which never hurts me, is so good a substitute that I am perfectly well satisfied upon that head. Less easy, however, do I find it to reconcile myself to an almost total abstinence from all vegetables, which yet I have been obliged to practise for some time. But enough, and too much by half, upon a subject that shall never again engross so large a portion of the paper that I devote to you.

You supposed in a former letter that Mrs. Cowper, of Devonshire Street, has written to me since I saw the rest of the family. Not so, my dear. Whatever intelligence she gave you concerning me, she had it from the Newtons, whom she visits. Yourself were the last of my female relations that I saw before I went to St. Alban's. You do not forget, I dare say, that you and Sir Thomas called upon me in my chamber a very few days before I took leave of London; then it was that I saw you last, and then it was that I said in my heart, upon your going out at the door, Farewell! there will be no more intercourse between us forever. But Providence has ordered otherwise, and I cannot help saying once more how sincerely I rejoice that he has. It were pity that, while the same world holds us, we, who were in a manner brought up together, should not love each other to the last. We do, however, and we do so in spite of a long separation; and although that separation should be for life, yet will we love each other.

I intended to have been very merry when I began, but I stumbled unawares upon a subject that made me otherwise; but if I have been a little sad, yet not disagreeably so to myself. That you admire Mr.

Pitt, my dear, may be, for aught I know, as you say it is, a very shining part of your character; but a more illustrious part of it, in my account, is your kindness and affection to me. Sweet self, you know, will always claim a right to be first considered, — a claim which few people are much given to dispute. Upon the subject of politics you may make me just what you please. I am perfectly prepared to adopt all your opinions; for living when and as I do, it is impossible that I should have any decided ones of my own. My mind, therefore, is as much a *carte blanche* in this particular as you can wish. Write upon it what you please. I know well that I honored his father, and that I have cut capers before now for victories obtained under his auspices; and although capering opportunities have become scarce since he died, yet I am equally ready even now to caper for his son when a reasonable occasion should offer. As to the King, I love and honor him upon a hundred accounts; and have, indeed, but one quarrel with him in the world, which is, that after having hunted a noble and beautiful animal till he takes it perhaps at last in a lady's parlor, he in a few days turns it up and hunts it again. When stags are followed by such people as generally follow them, it is very well: their pursuers are men who do not pretend to much humanity, and when they discover none, they are perfectly consistent with themselves; but I have a far different opinion of the character of our King: he is a merciful man, and should therefore be more merciful to his beast.

I admire and applaud your forgery; but your last

was performed in such haste that the date did not much resemble the direction. I imagine, however, that, all things considered, the Post Office, should they detect your contrivance, would not be much disposed to take notice of it. It is a common practice, but seldom so justifiably practised as by you.[1]

My dearest cousin, if you give me wine, there is no good reason wherefore you should also be at the expense of bottles, of which we could not possibly make any other use than to furnish the rack with them, where the cats will break them. I purpose, therefore, to return the hamper charged with the same number that it brings, by your permission. The difference will be sixteen shillings in the price of the wine.

Our post comes in on Wednesdays, Fridays, and Sundays; on the two former days about breakfast time, and on Sundays, at this season at least, in the afternoon. Adieu, my dear; I am never happier, I think, than when I am reading your letters, or answering them.

    Ever yours.

---

[1] The letter, no doubt, was franked in her father's name.

LVIII.

REASONS FOR TRANSLATING HOMER. — HOPE OF BETTER DAYS.

To the Rev. John Newton.

December 3, 1785.

MY DEAR FRIEND, — I am glad to hear that there is such a demand for your last Narrative. If I may judge of their general utility by the effect that they have heretofore had upon me, there are few things more edifying than death-bed memoirs. They interest every reader, because they speak of a period at which all must arrive, and afford a solid ground of encouragement to survivors to expect the same or similar support and comfort when it shall be their turn to die.

I also am employed in writing narrative, but not so useful. Employment, however, and with the pen, is, through habit, become essential to my well-being; and to produce always original poems, especially of considerable length, is not so easy. For some weeks after I had finished "The Task," and sent away the last sheet corrected, I was through necessity idle, and suffered not a little in my spirits for being so. One day, being in such distress of mind as was hardly supportable, I took up the Iliad; and merely to divert attention, and with no more preconception of what I was then entering upon than I have at this moment of what I shall be doing this day twenty years hence, translated the twelve first lines of it. The same necessity pressing me again, I had recourse to the same expedient, and translated more. Every day bringing its occasion for employment with it, every day consequently added something to the work; till at last I began to reflect thus: The Iliad and Odyssey together consist of about forty thousand verses. To translate these forty thousand verses will furnish me with occupation for a considerable time. I have already made some progress, and I find it a most agreeable amusement. Homer, in point of purity, is a most blameless writer; and though he was not an enlightened man, has interspersed many great and valuable truths throughout both his poems. In short, he is in all respects a most venerable old gentleman, by an acquaintance with whom no man can disgrace himself. The *literati* are all agreed, to a man, that although Pope has given us two pretty poems under Homer's titles, there is not to be found in them the least portion of Homer's spirit, nor the least resemblance of his manner. I will try, therefore, whether I cannot copy him somewhat more happily myself. I have at least the advantage of Pope's faults and failings, which, like so many buoys upon a dangerous coast, will serve me to steer by, and will make my chance for success more probable. These and many other considerations, but especially a mind that abhorred a vacuum as its chief bane, impelled me so effectually to the work that ere long I mean to publish proposals for a subscription to it, having advanced so far as to be warranted in doing so. I have connections, and no few such, by means of which I have the utmost reason to expect that a brisk circulation may be procured; and if it should prove a profitable enterprise, the profit will not accrue to a man who may be said not to want it. It is a business such as it will not, indeed, lie much in your way to promote; but among your numerous connections it is possible that you may know some who would sufficiently interest themselves in such a work to be not unwilling to subscribe to it. I do not mean — far be it from me — to put you upon making hazardous applications where you might possibly incur a refusal that would give you, though but a moment's, pain. You know best your own opportunities and powers in such a cause. If you can do but little, I shall esteem it much; and if you can do nothing, I am sure that it will not be for want of a will.

I have lately had three visits from my old schoolfellow, Mr. Bagot, a brother of Lord Bagot and of Mr. Chester of Chichely. At his last visit he brought his wife with him, a most amiable woman, to see Mrs. Unwin. I told him my purpose, and my progress. He received the news with great pleasure; immediately subscribed a draft of twenty pounds; and promised me his whole heart and his whole interest, which lies principally among people of the first fashion.

My correspondence has lately also been renewed with my dear cousin Lady Hesketh, whom I ever loved as a sister (for we were in a manner brought up together), and who writes to me as affectionately as if she were so. She also enters into my views and interests upon this occasion with a warmth that gives me great encouragement. The circle of *her* acquaintance is likewise very extensive; and I have no doubt that she will exert her influence to its utmost possibilities among them. I have other strings to my bow (perhaps, as a translator of Homer, I should say to my lyre), which I cannot here enumerate; but, upon the whole, my prospect seems promising enough. I have not yet consulted Johnson upon the occasion, but intend to do it soon.

My spirits are somewhat better than they were. In the course of the last month I have perceived a very sensible amendment. The hope of better days seems again to dawn upon me; and I have now and then an intimation, though slight and transient, that God has not abandoned me forever.

We have paid Nat. Gee his interest, and I enclose his acknowledgment. His last was so effectually mislaid that we have never found it. Mrs. Unwin, who sends her love, begs that you will pay out of that sum for the newspapers, and remit, if you can think of it, the few shillings that will remain, by the first that shall call upon you in his way to Olney. She is sorry that she forgot the greens.

This last paragraph must be considered as in a parenthesis, for I am going back to the subject of the preceding, viz., myself. Having been for some years troubled with an inconvenient stomach; and lately, with a stomach that will digest nothing without help; and we having reached the bottom of our own medical skill, into which we have dived to little or no purpose, — I have at length consented to consult Dr. Kerr, and expect to see him in a day or two. Engaged as I am, and am likely to be, so long as I am capable of it, in writing for the press, I cannot well afford to entertain a malady that is such an enemy to all mental operations.

The morning is beautiful, and tempts me forth into the garden. It is all the walk that I can have at this season, but not all the exercise. I ring a peal every day upon the dumb-bells.

I am, my dear friend, most truly,
Yours and Mrs. Newton's.

LIX.

PERSONAL EFFORTS IN BEHALF OF HOMER SUBSCRIPTIONS.

To the Rev. William Unwin.

December 31, 1785.

MY DEAR WILLIAM, — You have learned from my last that I am now conducting myself upon the plan that you recommended to me in the summer. But since I wrote it, I have made still farther advances in my negotiation with Johnson. The proposals are adjusted. The proof-sheet has been printed off, corrected, and returned. They will be sent abroad as soon as I can make up a complete list of the personages and persons to whom I would have them sent, which in a few days I hope to be able to accomplish. Johnson behaves very well, at least according to my conception of the matter, and seems sensible that I have dealt liberally with him. He wishes me to be a gainer by my labors, in his own words, "to put something handsome in my pocket," and recommends two large quartos for the whole. He would not (he says) by any means advise an extravagant price, and has fixed it at three guineas, — the half, as usual, to be paid at the time of subscribing, the remainder on delivery. Five hundred names (he adds) at this price will put above a thousand pounds into my purse. I am doing my best to obtain them. I have written, I think, to all my quondam friends, except those that are dead, requiring their assistance. I have gulped and swallowed, and I have written to the Chancellor, and I have written to Colman. I now bring them both to a fair test. They can both serve me most materially if so disposed. Mr. Newton is warm in my service, and can do not a little. I have of course written to Mr. Bagot, who, when he was here, with much earnestness and affection entreated me so to do, as soon as I should have settled the conditions. If I could get Sir Richard Sutton's address, I would write to him also, though I have been but once in his company since I left Westminster, where he and I read the Iliad and Odyssey through together. I enclose Lord Dartmouth's answer to my application, which I will get you to show to Lady Hesketh, because it will please her. I shall be glad if you can make an opportunity to call on her during your present stay in town. You observe therefore that I am not wanting to myself; he that is so, has no just claim on the assistance of others, neither shall myself have any cause to complain of me in other respects. I thank you for your friendly hints and precautions, and shall not fail to give them the guidance of my pen. I respect the public, and respect myself, and had rather want bread than expose myself wantonly to the condemnation of either. I hate the affectation, so frequently found in authors, of negligence and slovenly slightness; and in the present case am sensible how especially necessary it is to shun them, when I undertake the vast and invidious labor of doing better than Pope has done before me. I thank you for all that you have said and done in my cause, and beforehand for all that you shall say and do hereafter. I am sure that there will be no deficiency on your part. In particular, I thank you for taking such jealous care of my honor and respectability when the man you mention applied for samples of my translation. When I deal in wine, cloth, or cheese, I will give samples, but of verse never. No consideration would have induced me to comply with the gentleman's demand, unless he could have assured me that his wife had longed.

I have frequently thought with pleasure of the summer that you have had in your heart while you have been employed in softening the severity of winter in behalf of so many who must otherwise have been exposed to it. I wish that you could make a general jail-delivery, leaving only those behind who cannot elsewhere be so properly disposed of. You never said a better thing in your life than when you assured Mr. Smith of the expediency of a gift of bedding to the poor of Olney. There is no one article of this world's comforts with which, as Falstaff says, they are so heinously unprovided. When a poor woman, and an honest one, whom we know well, carried home two pair of blankets, a pair for herself and husband, and a pair for her six children, — as soon as the children saw them, they jumped out of their straw, caught them in their arms, kissed them, blessed them, and danced for joy. An old woman, a very old one, the first night that she found herself so comfortably covered, could not sleep a wink, being kept awake by the contrary emotions, of transport on the one hand, and the fear of not being thankful enough on the other.

It just occurs to me to say that this manuscript of mine will be ready for the press, as I hope, by the end of February. I shall have finished the Iliad in about ten days, and shall proceed immediately to the revisal of the whole. You must, if possible come down to Olney, if it be only that you may take the charge of its safe delivery to Johnson. For if by any accident it should be lost, I am undone, — the first copy being but a lean counterpart of the second.

Your mother joins with me in love and good wishes of every kind to you and all yours.

Adieu.

LX.

REVIEW OF IMPORTANT INCIDENTS IN HIS PAST LIFE.

To Lady Hesketh.

January 16, 1786.

MY DEAREST COUSIN, — I have sent, as I hope you have heard by this time, a specimen to my good friend the general.[1] To tell you the truth, I begin to be ashamed of myself that I had opposed him in the only two measures he recommended, and then assured him that I should be glad of his advice at all times. Having put myself under a course of strict self-examination upon this subject, I found at last that all the reluctance I had felt against a compliance with his wishes proceeded from a principle of shamefacedness at bottom that had insensibly influenced my reasonings, and determined me against the counsel of a man whom I knew to be wiser than myself. Wonderful as it may seem, my cousin, yet it is equally true that although I certainly did translate the Iliad with a design to publish it when I had done, and although I have twice issued from the press already, yet I do tremble at the thought, and so tremble at it that I could not bear to send out a specimen, because, by doing so, I should appear in public a good deal sooner than I had purposed. Thus have I developed my whole heart to you, and if you should think it at all expedient, have not the least objection to your communicating to the general this interpretation of the matter. The specimen has suffered a little through my too great zeal of amendment; in one instance, at least, it will be necessary to restore the original reading. And, by the way, I will observe that a scrupulous nicety is a dangerous thing. It often betrays a writer into a worse mistake than it

[1] Lady Hesketh had been the means of renewing the communication between Cowper and their kinsman, General Cowper. The "specimen" sent was part of the interview between Priam and Achilles, in the last book of the Iliad.

corrects, sometimes makes a blemish where before there was none, and is almost always fatal to the spirit of the performance.

You do not ask me, my dear, for an explanation of what I could mean by *anguish of mind* and by *the perpetual interruptions* that I mentioned. Because you *do not* ask, and because your reason for not asking consists of a delicacy and tenderness peculiar to yourself, for that very cause I will tell you. A wish so suppressed is more irresistible than many wishes plainly uttered. Know, then, that in the year 73 the same scene that was acted at St. Alban's opened upon me again at Olney, only covered with a still deeper shade of melancholy, and ordained to be of much longer duration. I was suddenly reduced from my wonted rate of understanding to an almost childish imbecility. I did not indeed lose my senses, but I lost the power to exercise them. I could return a rational answer even to a difficult question, but a question was necessary, or I never spoke at all. This state of mind was accompanied, as I suppose it to be in most instances of the kind, with misapprehension of things and persons that made me a very untractable patient. I believed that everybody hated me, and that Mrs. Unwin hated me most of all; was convinced that all my food was poisoned, together with ten thousand megrims of the same stamp. I would not be more circumstantial than is necessary. Dr. Cotton was consulted. He replied that he could do no more for me than might be done at Olney, but recommended particular vigilance, lest I should attempt my life, — a caution for which there was the greatest occasion. At the same time that I was convinced of Mrs. Unwin's aversion to me, I could endure no other companion. The whole management of me consequently devolved upon her, and a terrible task she had; she performed it, however, with a cheerfulness hardly ever equalled on such an occasion; and I have often heard her say that if ever she praised God in her life, it was when she found that she was to have all the labor. She performed it accordingly, but, as I hinted once before, very much to the hurt of her own constitution. It will be thirteen years in little more than a week since this malady seized me. Methinks I hear you ask, — your affection for me will, I know, make you wish to do so, — Is it removed? I reply, In great measure, but not quite. Occasionally I am much distressed, but that distress becomes continually less frequent, and I think less violent. I find writing, and especially poetry, my best remedy. Perhaps, had I understood music, I had never written verse, but had lived upon fiddle-strings instead. It is better, however, as it is. A poet may, if he pleases, be of a little use in the world, while a musician, the most skilful, can only divert himself and a few others. I have been emerging gradually from this pit. As soon as I became capable of action, I commenced carpenter, made cupboards, boxes, stools. I grew weary of this in about a twelvemonth, and addressed myself to the making of birdcages. To this employment succeeded that of gardening, which I intermingled with that of drawing; but finding that the latter occupation injured my eyes, I renounced it, and commenced poet. I have given you, my dear, a little history in shorthand; I know that it will touch your feelings, but do not let it interest them too much. *In the year when I wrote " The Task"* (for it occupied me about a year) *I was very often most supremely unhappy*, and am under God indebted in good part to that work for not having been much worse. You did not know what a clever fellow I am, and how I can turn my hand to anything.

I perceive that this time I shall make you pay double postage, and there is no help for it. Unless I write myself out now, I shall forget half of what I have to say. Now, therefore, for the interruptions at which I hinted. — There came a lady into this country, by name and title Lady Austen, the widow of the late Sir Robert Austen. At first she lived with her sister, about a mile from Olney; but in a few weeks took lodgings at the vicarage here. Between the vicarage and the back of our house are interposed our garden, an orchard, and the garden belonging to the vicarage. She had lived much in France, was very sensible, and had infinite vivacity. She took a great liking to us, and we to her. She had been used to a great deal of company, and we, fearing that she would find such a transition into silent retirement irksome, contrived to give her our agreeable company often. Becoming continually more and more intimate, a practice obtained at length of our dining with each other alternately every day, Sundays excepted. In order to facilitate our communication, we made doors in the two garden-walls above said, by which means we considerably shortened the way from one house to the other, and could meet when we pleased without entering the town at all, — a measure the rather expedient because in winter the town is abominably dirty, and she kept no carriage. On her first settlement in our neighborhood I made it my particular business (for at that time I was not employed in writing, having published my first volume, and not begun my second) to pay my devoirs to her ladyship every morning at eleven. Customs very soon become laws. I began "The Task," — for she was the lady who gave me the Sofa for a subject. Being once engaged in the work, I began to feel the inconvenience of my morning attendance. We had seldom breakfasted ourselves till ten, and the intervening hour was all the time that I could find in the whole day for writing; and occasionally it would happen that the half of that hour was all that I could secure for the purpose. But there was no remedy; long usage had made that which at first was optional, a point of good manners, and consequently of necessity, and I was forced to neglect "The Task" to attend upon the Muse who had inspired the subject. But she had ill health, and before I quite finished the work was obliged to repair to Bristol. Thus, as I told you, my dear, the cause of the many interruptions that I mentioned, was removed, and now, except the Bull that I spoke of, we have seldom any company at all. After all that I have said upon this matter, you will not completely understand me, perhaps, unless I account for the remainder of the day. I will add, therefore, that having paid my morning visit, I walked; returning from my walk, I dressed; we then met and dined, and parted not till between ten and eleven at night.

My cousin, I thank you for giving me a copy of the general's note, of which I and my publication were so much the subject. I learned from it, better than I could have learned the same thing from any other document, the kindness of his purposes towards me, and how much I may depend on his assistance. I am vexed, and have been these three days, that I thwarted him in the affair of a specimen;[1] but as I told you, I have still my gloomy hours, which had their share, together with the more powerful cause assigned above, in determining my behavior. But I have given the best proof possible of my repentance, and was indeed in such haste to evince it that I sent my despatches to Newport, on purpose to catch the by-post. How much—I—love you for the generosity of that offer which made the general observe that your money seemed to burn in your pocket, I cannot readily, nor indeed at all, express. Neither is Mrs. Unwin in the least behind me in her sense of it. We may well admire and love you, for we have not met with many such occurrences, or even heard of many such, since we first entered a world where friendship is in every mouth, but finds only here and there a heart that has room for it.

I know well, my cousin, how formidable a creature you are when you become once outrageous. No sprat in a storm is half so terrible. But it is all in vain. You are at a distance, so we snap our fingers at you. Not that we have any more fowls at pres-

[1] Having at first refused the request to send a specimen.

ent. No, no; you may make yourself easy upon that subject. The coop is empty, and at this time of year cannot be replenished; but the spring will soon begin to advance. There are such things as eggs in the world, which eggs will, by incubation, be transformed, some of them into chickens, and others of them into ducklings. So muster up all your patience, for as sure as you live, if we live also, we shall put it to the trial. But, seriously, you must not deny us one of the greatest pleasures we can have, which is to give you now and then a little tiny proof how much we value you. We cannot sit with our hands before us and be contented with only saying that we love Lady Hesketh.

The little item that you inserted in your cover, concerning a review of a certain author's work, in the "Gentleman's Magazine," excited Mrs. Unwin's curiosity to see it in a moment. In vain did I expostulate with her on the vanity of all things here below, especially of human praise, telling her what perhaps indeed she had heard before, but what on such an occasion I thought it not amiss to remind her of, that at the best it is but as the idle wind that whistles as it passes by, and that a little attention to the dictates of reason would presently give her the victory over all the curiosity that she felt so troublesome. For a short time, indeed, I prevailed, but the next day the fit returned upon her with more violence than before. She would see it, — she was resolved that she would see it that moment. You must know, my dear, that a watchmaker lives within two or three doors of us, who takes in the said Magazine for a gentleman at some distance, and as it happened it had not been sent to its proper owner. Accordingly, the messenger that the lady despatched, returned with it, and she was gratified. As to myself, I read the article indeed, and read it to her; but I do not concern myself much, you may suppose, about such matters, and shall only make two or three cursory remarks, and so conclude. In the first place, therefore, I observe that it is enough to craze a poor poet to see his verses so miserably misprinted, and, which is worse, if possible, his very praises in a manner annihilated, by a jumble of the lines out of their places, so that in two instances the end of the period takes the lead of the beginning of it. The said poet has still the more reason to be crazed because the said Magazine is in general singularly correct. But at Christmas, no doubt, your printer will get drunk as well as another man. It is astonishing to me that they know so exactly how much I translated of Voltaire. My recollection, refreshed by them, tells me that they are right in the number of the books that they affirm to have been translated by me, but till they brought the fact again to my mind, I myself had forgotten that part of the business entirely. My brother had twenty guineas for eight books of English "Henriade," and I furnished him with four of them. They are not equally accurate in the affair of the Tame Mouse. That I kept one is certain, and that I kept it, as they say, in my bureau, — but not in the Temple; it was while I was at Westminster. I kept it till it produced six young ones, and my transports when I first discovered them cannot easily be conceived, — any more than my mortification when, going again to visit my little family, I found that mouse herself had eaten them! I turned her loose, in indignation, and vowed never to keep a mouse again. Who the writer of this article can be, I am not able to imagine, nor where he had his information of these particulars. But they know all the world and everything that belongs to it. The mistake that has occasioned the mention of Unwin's name in the margin would be ludicrous if it were not inadvertently, indeed, and innocently on their part profane. I should have thought it impossible that when I spoke of One who had been wounded in the hands and in the side, any reader in a Christian land could have been for a moment at a loss for the person intended.

Adieu, my dear cousin; I intended that one of these should have served as a case for the other, but before I was aware of it I filled both sheets completely. However, as your money burns in your pocket, there is no harm done. I shall not add a syllable more, except that I am, and while I breathe ever shall be,

              Most truly yours.

LXI.

ARRANGEMENTS FOR HIS COUSIN'S COMING TO OLNEY. — HOMER. — THE CRITICS.

To Lady Hesketh.

OLNEY, *February* 19, 1786.

MY DEAREST COUSIN, — Since so it must be, so it shall be. If you will not sleep under the roof of a friend, may you never sleep under the roof of an enemy! An enemy, however, you will not presently find. Mrs. Unwin bids me mention her affectionately, and tell you that she willingly gives up a part, for the sake of the rest, — willingly, at least, as far as willingly may consist with some reluctance. I feel my reluctance too. Our design was, that you should have slept in the room that serves me for a study; and its having been occupied by you would have been an additional recommendation of it to me. But all reluctances are superseded by the thought of seeing you; and because we have nothing so much at heart as the wish to see you happy and comfortable, we are desirous, therefore, to accommodate you to your own mind, and not to ours. Mrs. Unwin has already secured for you an apartment, or rather two, just such as we could wish. The house in which you will find them is within thirty yards of our own, and opposite to it. The whole affair is thus commodiously adjusted; and now I have nothing to do but to wish for June; and June, my cousin, was never so wished for since

June was made. I shall have a thousand things to hear, and a thousand to say, and they will all rush into my mind together, till it will be so crowded with things impatient to be said that for some time I shall say nothing. But no matter, — sooner or later they will all come out; and since we shall have you the longer for not having you under our own roof (a circumstance that, more than anything, reconciles us to that measure), they will stand the better chance. After so long a separation, a separation that of late seemed likely to last for life, we shall meet each other as alive from the dead; and for my own part, I can truly say that I have not a friend in the other world whose resurrection would give me greater pleasure.

I am truly happy, my dear, in having pleased you with what you have seen of my Homer. I wish that all English readers had your unsophisticated, or rather unadulterated, taste, and could relish simplicity like you. But I am well aware that in this respect I am under a disadvantage, and that many, especially many ladies, missing many turns and prettinesses of expression that they have admired in Pope, will account my translation in those particulars defective. But I comfort myself with the thought that in reality it is no defect; on the contrary, that the want of all such embellishments as do not belong to the original will be one of its principal merits with persons indeed capable of relishing Homer. He is the best poet that ever lived for many reasons, but for none more than for that majestic plainness that distinguishes him from all others. As an accomplished person moves gracefully without thinking of it, in like manner the dignity of Homer seems to cost him no labor. It was natural to him to say great things, and to say them well, and little ornaments were beneath his notice. If Maty,[1] my dearest cousin, should return to you my copy with any such strictures as may make it necessary for me to see it again before it goes to Johnson, in that case you shall send it to me, otherwise to Johnson immediately; for he writes me word he wishes his friend[2] to go to work upon it as soon as possible. When you come, my dear, we will hang all these critics together, for they have worried me without remorse or conscience, — at least one of them has. I had actually murdered more than a few of the best lines in the specimen, in compliance with his requisitions, but plucked up my courage at last, and in the very last opportunity that I had, recovered them to life again by restoring the original reading. At the same time I readily confess that the specimen is the better for all this discipline its author has undergone; but then it has been more indebted for its improvement to that pointed accuracy of examination to which I was myself excited, than to any proposed amendments from Mr. Critic; for as sure as you are my cousin whom I long to see at Olney, so surely would he have done me irreparable mischief, if I would have given him leave.

[1] Dr. Maty, of the "Museum," who wrote the review of "The Task" for that periodical.

[2] Fuseli, whose accurate acquaintance with the original proved of great service to the translation.

My friend Bagot writes to me in a most friendly strain, and calls loudly upon me for original poetry. When I shall have done with Homer, probably he will not call in vain. Having found the prime feather of a swan on the banks of the *smug and silver Trent*, he keeps it for me.

Adieu, my dear cousin.

I am sorry that the general has such indifferent health. He must not die. I can by no means spare a person so kind to me.

LXII.

LODGING-HUNTING; PART OF THE VICARAGE SECURED.

To Lady Hesketh.

Monday, April 10, 1786.

THAT'S my good cousin! now I love you! now I will think of June as you do, that it is the pleasantest of all months, unless you should happen to be here in November too, and make it equally delightful. Before I shall have finished my letter, Mrs. Unwin will have taken a view of the house concerning which you inquire, and I shall be able to give you a circumstantial account of it. The man who built it is lately dead; he had been a common sailor, and assisted, under Wolfe and Amherst, at the taking of Quebec. When we came hither he was almost penniless; but climbing by degrees into the lace business, amassed money, and built the house in question. Just before he died, having an enterprising genius, he put almost his whole substance to hazard in sending a large cargo of lace to America, and the venture failing, he has left his widow in penury and distress. For this reason I conclude that she will have no objection to letting as much of her house as my cousin will have occasion for, and have therefore given you this short history of the matter. The bed is the best in the town; and the honest tar's folly was much laughed at when it was known that he, who had so often swung in a hammock, had given twenty pounds for a bed. But now I begin to hope that he made a wiser bargain than I once thought it. She is no gentlewoman, as you may suppose, but she is nevertheless a very quiet, decent, sober body, and well respected among her neighbors.

But Hadley, my dearest cousin, what is to be said of Hadley? Only this at present, that having such an inhabitant as Mr. Burrows, and the hope belonging to it of such another inhabitant as yourself, it has all charms, all possible recommendations. Yes; had I the wings that David wished for, I would surely stretch them to their utmost extent, that I might reach any place where I should have you to converse with perhaps half the year. But alas! my dear, instead of wings, I have a chain and a collar; the history of which collar and chain Mrs. Unwin shall give you when you come, else I would fly, and she would fly also, with the utmost alacrity to Hadley, or whithersoever you should call us, for Olney has no hold upon us in particular. Here have we no family connections, no neighbors with whom we can associate, no friendships. If the country is pleasant, so also are other countries; and so far as income is concerned, we should not, I suppose, find ourselves in a more expensive situation at Hadley, or anywhere, than here. But there are lets and hindrances which no power of man can remove, which will make your poor heart ache, my dear, when you come to know them. I will not say that they can never be removed, because I will not set bounds to that which has no bounds, — the mercy of God; but of the removal of them there is no present apparent probability. I knew a Mr. Burrows once, — it was when I lived in the Temple; so far knew him that we simpered at each other when we met, and on opposite sides of the way touched hats. This Mr. Burrows, though at that time a young man, was rather remarkable for corpulence, and yet tall. He was at the bar. On a sudden I missed him, and was informed soon after that he had taken orders. Is it possible that your Mr. Burrows and mine can be the same? The imagination is not famous for taking good likenesses of persons and faces that we never saw. In general, the picture that we draw in our minds of an *inconnu* is of all possible pictures the most unlike the original. So it has happened to me in this instance; my fancy assured me that Mr. Burrows was a slim, elegant young man, dressed always to the very point of exactness, with a sharp face, a small voice, a delicate address, and the gentlest manners.

Such was my dream of Mr. Burrows; and how my dream of him came to be such I know not, unless it arose from what I seemed to have collected out of the several letters in which you have mentioned him. From them I learned that he has wit, sense, taste, and genius, with which qualities I do not generally connect the ideas of bulk and rotundity; and from them I also learned that he has numerous connections at your end of the town, where the company of those who have anything rough in their exterior is least likely to be coveted. So it must have come to pass that I made to myself such a very unsuitable representation of him. But I am not sorry that he is such as he is; he is no loser by the bargain, in my account. I am not the less delighted with his high approbation, and wish for no better fortune as a poet than always so to please such men as Mr. Burrows. I will not say, my dear, that you yourself gain any advantage in my opinion by the difference, for to seat you higher there than you were always seated is not possible. I will only observe in this instance, as always in all instances, I discover a proof of your own good sense and discernment, who, finding in Mr. Burrows a mind so deserving of your esteem and regard, have not suffered your eye to prejudice you against it, — a *faux pas* into which I have known ladies of very good understanding betrayed ere now, I assure you. Had there been a question last year of our meeting at Olney, I should have felt myself particularly interested in this inattention of yours to the figure, for the sake of its contents; for at that time I had rather more body than it became a man who pretends to public approbation as a poet to carry about him. But, thanks to Dr. Kerr, I do not at present measure an inch more in the girth than is perfectly consistent with the highest pretensions in that way. Apollo himself is hardly less chargeable with prominence about the waist than I am.

I by no means insist upon making ladies of the Trojan women, unless I can reconcile you to the term. But I must observe, in the first place, that though in our language the word be of modern use, it is likewise very ancient. We read in our oldest Bibles of the elect *Lady*, and of Babylon, the *Lady* of kingdoms. In the next place, the Grecians, Homer at least, when a woman of rank is accosted, takes care in many instances that she shall be addressed in a style suited to her condition; for which purpose he employs a word more magnificent in its amount than even lady, and which literally signifies very little less than goddess. The word that I mean — that I may make it legible to you — is *Daimonie*. There were, no doubt, in Troy — But I will say no more of it. I have that to write about to my English lady that makes all the ladies of antiquity nothing worth to me.

We are at this moment returned from the house above mentioned. The parlor is small and neat, not a mere cupboard, but very passable; the chamber is better, and quite smart. There is a little room close to your own for Mrs. Eaton, and there is room for Cookee and Samuel. The terms are half a guinea a week; but it seems as if we were never to take a step without a stumble. The kitchen is bad, — it has, indeed, never been used except as a washhouse; for people at Olney do not eat and drink as they do in other places. I do not mean, my dear, that they quaff nectar or feed on ambrosia, but *tout au contraire.* So what must be done about this abominable kitchen? It is out of doors, — that is not amiss. It has neither range nor jack, — that is terrible. But then range and jack are not unattainables; they may be easily supplied. And if it were not — abominable kitchen that it is — no bigger than half an egg-shell, shift might be made. The good woman is content that your servants should eat and drink in her parlor, but expects that they shall disperse themselves when they have done. But whither, who can say? — unless into the arbor in the garden; for that they should solace themselves in said kitchen were hardly to be expected. While I write this, Mrs. U. is gone to attempt a treaty with the linendraper over the way, which, if she succeeds, will be best of all, because the rooms are better, and it is just at hand. I must halt till she returns. — She returns, — nothing done. She is gone again to another place; once more I halt. Again she returns, and opens the parlor door with these tidings: " I have succeeded beyond my utmost hopes. I went to Maurice Smith's (he, you must know, my dear, is a Jack-of-all-trades); I said, 'Do you know if Mr. Brightman could and would let lodgings ready furnished to a lady with three servants?' Maurice's wife calls out (she is a Quaker), 'Why dost thee not take the vicarage?' I replied, 'There is no furniture.' 'Pshaw!' quoth Maurice's wife; 'we will furnish it for thee, and at the lowest rate; from a bed to a platter, we will find all.'" "And what do you intend now?" said I to Mrs. Unwin. "Why, now," quoth she, "I am going to the curate to hear what *he* says." So away she goes, and in about twenty minutes returns. "Well, now it is all settled. Lady H. is to have all the vicarage, except two rooms, at the rate of ten guineas a year; and Maurice will furnish it for five guineas from June to November, inclusive." So, my dear, you and your train are provided for to my heart's content. They are Lady Austen's lodgings, only with more room, and at the same price. You have a parlor sixteen feet by fourteen, chamber ditto; a room for your own maid, near to your own, that I have occupied many a good time; an exceeding good garret for Cookee, and another ditto, at a convenient distance, for Samuel; a cellar, a good kitchen, the use of the garden, — in short, all that you can want. Give us our commission in your next, and all shall be ready by the first of June. You will observe, my beloved cousin, that it is not in all above eight shillings a week in the whole year, or but a trifle more. And the furniture is really smart, and the beds good. But you must find your own linen. Come, then, my beloved cousin, for I am determined that, whatsoever king shall reign, you shall be *Vicar* of Olney. Come and cheer my heart. I have left many things unsaid, but shall note them another time. Adieu!

Ever yours.

I am so charmed with the subject that concludes my letter that I grudge every inch of paper to any other. Yet must I allow myself space to say that Lord Dartmouth's behavior to you at the concert has won my heart to him more than ever. It was such a well-timed kindness to me, and so evidently performed with an equal design of giving pleasure to you, that I love him for it at my heart. I have never, indeed, at any time had occasion to charge him, as I know that many have done, with want of warmth in his friendship. I honor you, my dear, for your constellation of nobles. I rejoice that the contents of my box have pleased you; may I never write anything that does not! My friend Bull brought me to-day the last "Gentleman's Magazine." There your cousin is held up again. Oh, rare coz!

LXIII.

DESCRIPTION OF THE VICARAGE.

To Lady Hesketh.

OLNEY, *April* 17, 1786.

MY DEAREST COUSIN, — If you will not quote Solomon, my dearest cousin, I will. He says, and as beautiful as truly: "Hope deferred maketh the heart sick, but when the desire cometh, it is a tree of life." I feel how much reason he had on his side when he made this observation, and am myself sick of your fortnight's delay.

The vicarage was built by Lord Dartmouth, and was not finished till some time after we arrived at Olney, consequently it is new. It is a smart stone building, well sashed, by much too good for the living, but just what I would wish for you. It has, as you justly concluded from my premises, a garden, but rather calculated for use than ornament. It is square and well walled, but has neither arbor nor alcove nor other shade except the shadow of the house. But we have two gardens, which are yours. Between your mansion and ours is interposed nothing but an orchard, into which a door opening out of our garden affords us the easiest communication imaginable, will save the roundabout by the town, and make both houses one. Your chamber-windows look over the river and over the meadows to a village called Emberton, and command the whole length of a long bridge described by a certain poet, together with a view of the road at a distance.[1] Should you wish for books at Olney, you must bring them with you, or you will wish in vain; for I have none but the works of a certain poet, — Cowper, of whom perhaps you have heard; and they are as yet but two volumes. They may multiply hereafter, but at present they are no more.

You are the first person for whom I have heard Mrs. Unwin express such feelings as she does for you. She is not profuse in professions, nor forward to enter into treaties of friendship with new faces; but when her friendship is once engaged, it may be confided in even unto death. She loves you already,

[1] See The Task, Book IV.

and how much more will she love you before this time twelvemonth! I have indeed endeavored to describe you to her; but perfectly as I have you by heart, I am sensible that my picture cannot do you justice. I never saw one that did. Be you what you may, you are much beloved, and will be so at Olney; and Mrs. U. expects you with the pleasure that one feels at the return of a long absent, dear relation, — that is to say, with a pleasure such as mine. She sends you her warmest affections.

On Friday I received a letter from dear Anonymous,[1] apprising me of a parcel that the coach would bring me on Saturday. Who is there in the world that has, or thinks he has, reason to love me to the degree that he does? But it is no matter, he chooses to be unknown; and his choice is, and ever shall be, so sacred to me that if his name lay on the table before me reversed, I would not turn the paper about that I might read it. Much as it would gratify me to thank him, I would turn my eyes away from the forbidden discovery. I long to assure him that those same eyes, concerning which he expresses such kind apprehensions lest they should suffer by this laborious undertaking, are as well as I could expect them to be if I were never to touch either book or pen. Subject to weakness and occasional slight inflammations it is probable that they will always be; but I cannot remember the time when they enjoyed anything so like an exemption from those infirmities as at present. One would almost suppose that reading Homer were the best ophthalmic in the world.

[1] Probably Theodora Cowper, his ever-faithful lady-love.

I should be happy to remove his solicitude on the subject; but it is a pleasure that he will not let me enjoy. Well, then, I will be content without it, — and so content that, though I believe you, my dear, to be in full possession of all this mystery, you shall never know me, while you live, either directly or by hints of any sort attempt to extort or to steal the secret from you. I should think myself as justly punishable as the Bethshemites for looking into the ark, which they were not allowed to touch.

I have not sent for Kerr,[1] for Kerr can do nothing but send me to Bath; and to Bath I cannot go for a thousand reasons. The summer will set me up again. I grow fat every day, and shall be as big as Gog or Magog, or both put together, before you come.

I did actually live three years with Mr. Chapman, a solicitor, — that is to say, I slept three years in his house; but I lived — that is to say, I spent my days — in Southampton Row, as you very well remember. There was I, and the future Lord Chancellor, constantly employed from morning to night in giggling and making giggle, instead of studying the law. Oh, fie! — cousin, how could you do so? I am pleased with Lord Thurlow's inquiries about me. If he takes it into that inimitable head of his, he may make a man of me yet. I could love him heartily if he would but deserve it at my hands. That I did so once is certain. The Duchess of ———, who in the world set her a-going? But if all the duchesses in the world were spinning like so many whirligigs for my benefit, I would not stop them. It is a noble

[1] Dr. Kerr of Northampton.

thing to be a poet, it makes all the world so lively. I might have preached more sermons than even Tillotson did, and better, and the world would have been still fast asleep; but a volume of verse is a fiddle that puts the universe in motion.

Yours, my dear friend and cousin.

LXIV.

JOY IN LETTERS. — COWPERSHIP.

To Lady Hesketh.

OLNEY, *April* 24, 1786.

YOUR letters are so much my comfort that I often tremble lest by any accident I should be disappointed, and the more because you have been more than once so engaged in company on the writing day that I have had a narrow escape. Let me give you a piece of good counsel, my cousin: follow my laudable example, — write when you can; take Time's forelock in one hand and a pen in the other, and so make sure of your opportunity. It is well for me that you write faster than anybody, and more in an hour than other people in two, else I know not what would become of me. When I read your letters, I hear you talk; and I love talking letters dearly, especially from you. Well, the middle of June will not be always a thousand years off; and when it comes I shall hear you, and see you too, and shall not care a farthing then if you do not touch a pen in a month.

By the way, you must either send me or bring me some more paper; for before the moon shall have performed a few more revolutions I shall not have a scrap left, — and tedious revolutions they are just now, that is certain.

I give you leave to be as peremptory as you please, especially at a distance; but when you say that you are a Cowper (and the better it is for the Cowpers that such you are, and I give them joy of you with all my heart), you must not forget that I boast myself a Cowper too, and have my humors and fancies and purposes and determinations as well as others of my name, and hold them as fast as they can. *You* indeed tell *me* how often I shall see you when you come, — a pretty story truly! I am a *he* Cowper, my dear, and claim the privileges that belong to my noble sex. But these matters shall be settled, as my cousin Agamemnon used to say, at a more convenient time.

I shall rejoice to see the letter you promise me; for though I met with a morsel of praise last week, I do not know that the week current is likely to produce me any, and having lately been pretty much pampered with that diet, I expect to find myself rather hungry by the time when your next letter shall arrive. It will therefore be very opportune. The morsel above alluded to came from — whom do you think? From ———; but she desires that her authorship may be a secret; and in my answer I promised not to divulge it, except to you. It is a pretty copy of verses, neatly written and well turned, and when you come you shall see them. I intend to keep all pretty things to myself till then, that they may serve me as a bait to lure you hither more effectually. The last letter that I had from ——— I received so many years since that it seems as if it had reached me a good while before I was born.

I was grieved at the heart that the general could not come, and that illness was in part the cause that hindered him. I have sent him, by his express desire, a new edition of the first book and half the second. He would not suffer me to send it to you, my dear, lest you should post it away to Maty at once. He did not give that reason; but being shrewd, I found it.

The grass begins to grow and the leaves to bud, and everything is preparing to be beautiful against you come. Adieu!

You inquire of our walks, I perceive, as well as of our rides: they are beautiful. You inquire also concerning a cellar: you have two cellars. Oh, what years have passed since we took the same walks and drank out of the same bottle! But a few more weeks, and then — !

LXV.

ANNOUNCING INTENDED REMOVAL TO WESTON.

To the Rev. William Unwin.

OLNEY, *July* 3, 1786.

MY DEAR WILLIAM, — After a long silence I begin again. A day given to my friends is a day taken from Homer; but to such an interruption now and then occurring I have no objection. Lady Hesketh is, as you observe, arrived, and has been with us near a fortnight. She pleases everybody, and is pleased in her turn with everything she finds at Olney; is always cheerful and sweet-tempered, and knows no pleasure equal to that of communicating pleasure to us, and to all around her. This disposition in her is the more comfortable because it is not the humor of the day, — a sudden flash of benevolence and good spirits occasioned merely by a change of scene, — but it is her natural turn, and has governed all her conduct ever since I knew her first. We are consequently happy in her society, and shall be happier still to have you to partake with us in our joy. I can now assure you that her complexion is not at all indebted to art, having seen a hundred times the most convincing proof of its authenticity, — her color fading and glowing again alternately as the weather or her own temperature has happened to affect it, while she has been sitting before me. I am fond of the sound of bells, but was never more pleased with those of Olney than when they rang her into her new habitation. It is a compliment that our performers upon those instruments have never paid to any other personage (Lord Dartmouth excepted) since we knew the town. In short, she is, as she ever was, my pride and my joy, and I am delighted with everything that means to do her honor. Her first appearance was too much for me. My spirits — instead of being greatly raised, as I had inadvertently supposed they would be — broke down with me under the pressure of too much joy, and left me flat, or rather melancholy, throughout the day, to a degree that was mortifying to myself, and alarming to her. But I have made amends for this failure since, and in point of cheerfulness have far exceeded her expectations; for she knew that sable had been my suit for many years.

And now I shall communicate intelligence that will give you pleasure. When you first contemplated the front of our abode you were shocked. In your eyes it had the appearance of a prison, and you sighed at the thought that your mother dwelt in it. Your view of it was not only just, but prophetic. It had not only the aspect of a place built for the purpose of incarceration, but has actually served that purpose through a long, long period, and we have been the prisoners. But a jail-delivery is at hand: the bolts and bars are to be loosed, and we shall escape. A very different mansion, both in point of appearance and accommodation, expects us, and the expense of living in it not greater than we are subjected to in this. It is situated at Weston, — one of the prettiest villages in England, — and belongs to Mr. Throckmorton. We all three dine with him to-day by invitation, and shall survey it in the afternoon, point out the necessary repairs, and finally adjust the treaty. I have my cousin's promise that she will never let another year pass without a visit to us; and the house is large enough to contain us and our suite and her also, with as many of hers as she shall choose to bring. The change will, I hope, prove advantageous both to your mother and me in all respects. Here we have no neighborhood; there we shall have most agreeable neighbors in the Throckmortons. Here we have a bad air in winter, impregnated with the fishy smelling fumes of the marsh miasma; there we shall breathe in an atmosphere untainted. Here we are confined from September to March, and sometimes longer; there we shall be upon the very verge of pleasure-grounds in which we can always ramble, and shall not wade through almost impassable dirt to get at them. Both your mother's constitution and mine have suffered materially by such close and long confinement; and it is high time, unless we intend to retreat into the grave, that we should seek out a more wholesome residence. A pretty deal of new furniture will be wanted, especially chairs and beds, — all which my kind cousin will provide, and fit up a parlor and a chamber for herself into the bargain. So far is well; the rest is left to Heaven.

I have hardly left myself room for an answer to your queries concerning my friend John and his studies. What the supplement of Hirtius is made of, I know not; we did not read it at Westminster. I should imagine it might be dispensed with. I should recommend the Civil War of Cæsar, because he wrote it, — who ranks, I believe, as the best writer, as well as soldier, of his day. There are books (I know not what they are, but you do, and can easily find them) that will inform him clearly of both the civil and military management of the Romans, — the several officers, I mean, in both departments, and what was the peculiar province of each. The study of some such book would, I should think, prove a good introduction to that of Livy, unless you have a Livy with notes to that effect. A want of intelligence in those points has heretofore made the Roman history very dark and difficult to me; therefore I thus advise.

Our love is with all your lovelies, both great and small.

Yours ever.

LXVI.

FUSELI. — HOMER. — DENNIS.

To the Rev. Walter Bagot.[1]

OLNEY, *July* 4, 1786.

I REJOICE, my dear friend, that you have at last received my proposals, and most cordially thank you for all your labors in my service. I have friends in the world who, knowing that I am apt to be careless when left to myself, are determined to watch over me with a jealous eye upon this occasion. The consequence will be that the work will be better executed, but more tardy in the production. To them I owe it that my translation, as fast as it proceeds, passes under a revisal of the most accurate discerner of all blemishes. I know not whether I told you before, or now tell you for the first time, that I am in the hands of a very extraordinary person.[2] He is

---

[1] A friend of school-boy days at Westminster.
[2] Fuseli.

intimate with my bookseller, and voluntarily offered his service. I was at first doubtful whether to accept it or not; but finding that my friends abovesaid were not to be satisfied on any other terms, though myself a perfect stranger to the man and his qualifications, except as he was recommended by Johnson, I at length consented, and have since found great reason to rejoice that I did. I called him an extraordinary person, and such he is; for he is not only versed in Homer and accurate in his knowledge of the Greek to a degree that entitles him to that appellation, but, though a foreigner, is a perfect master of our language, and has exquisite taste in English poetry. By his assistance I have improved many passages, supplied many oversights, and corrected many mistakes, — such as will, of course, escape the most diligent and attentive laborer in such a work. I ought to add — because it affords the best assurance of his zeal and fidelity — that he does not toil for hire, nor will accept of any premium, but has entered on this business merely for his amusement. In the last instance my sheets will pass through the hands of our old schoolfellow Colman, who has engaged to correct the press and make any little alterations that he may see expedient. With all this precaution, little as I intended it once, I am now well satisfied. Experience has convinced me that other eyes than my own are necessary, in order that so long and arduous a task may be finished as it ought, and may neither discredit me nor mortify and disappoint my friends. You, who I know interest yourself much and deeply in my success, will I dare say be satisfied with it too. Pope had many aids; and he who follows Pope ought not to walk alone.

Though I announce myself by my very undertaking to be one of Homer's most enraptured admirers, I am not a blind one. Perhaps the speech of Achilles given in my specimen is, as you hint, rather too much in the moralizing strain to suit so young a man and of so much fire. But whether it be or not, in the course of the close application that I am forced to give to my author, I discover inadvertencies not a few, — some perhaps that have escaped even the commentators themselves, or perhaps in the enthusiasm of their idolatry they resolved that they should pass for beauties. Homer, however, say what they will, was man; and in all the works of man, especially in a work of such length and variety, many things will of necessity occur that might have been better. Pope and Addison had a Dennis; and Dennis, if I mistake not, held up as he has been to scorn and detestation, was a sensible fellow, and passed some censures upon both those writers that had they been less just would have hurt them less. Homer had his Zoilus; and perhaps if we knew all that Zoilus said, we should be forced to acknowledge that sometimes, at least, he had reason on his side. But it is dangerous to find any fault at all with what the world is determined to esteem faultless.

I rejoice, my dear friend, that you enjoy some composure and cheerfulness of spirits. May God preserve and increase to you so great a blessing!

I am affectionately and truly yours.

LXVII.

UNHEALTHFULNESS OF OLNEY. — STATE OF HIS MIND.

To the Rev. John Newton.

August 5, 1786.

MY DEAR FRIEND, — I am neither idle nor forgetful; on the contrary, I think of you often, and my thoughts would more frequently find their way to my pen, were I not of necessity every day occupied in Homer. This long business engrosses all my mornings, and when the days grow shorter will have all my evenings too; at present, they are devoted to walking, — an exercise to me as necessary as my food.

You have heard of our intended removal. The house that is to receive us is in a state of preparation, and when finished will be both smarter and more commodious than our present abode. But the circumstance that recommends it chiefly is its situation. Long confinement in the winter, and indeed for the most part in the autumn too, has hurt us both. A gravel walk, thirty yards long, affords but indifferent scope to the locomotive faculty; yet it is all that we have had to move in for eight months in the year, during thirteen years that I have been a prisoner. Had I been confined in the Tower, the battlements of it would have furnished me with a larger space. You say well that there was a time when I was happy at Olney; and I am now as happy at

Olney as I expect to be anywhere without the presence of God. Change of situation is with me no otherwise an object than as both Mrs. Unwin's health and mine may happen to be concerned in it. A fever of the slow and spirit-oppressing kind seems to belong to all, except the natives who have dwelt in Olney many years, — and the natives have putrid fevers. Both they and we, I believe, are immediately indebted for our respective maladies to an atmosphere incumbered with raw vapors issuing from flooded meadows; and we in particular, perhaps, have fared the worse for sitting so often, and sometimes for months, over a cellar filled with water. These ills we shall escape in the uplands, and as we may reasonably hope, of course, their consequences. But as for happiness, he that has once had communion with his Maker must be more frantic than ever I was yet, if he can dream of finding it at a distance from him. I no more expect happiness at Weston than here, or than I should expect it in company with felons and outlaws in the hold of a ballast-lighter. Animal spirits, however, have their value, and are especially desirable to him who is condemned to carry a burden, which at any rate will tire him, but which, without their aid, cannot fail to crush him; the dealings of God with me are to myself utterly unintelligible. I have never met, either in books or in conversation, with an experience at all similar to my own. More than a twelvemonth has passed since I began to hope that, having walked the whole breadth of the bottom of this Red Sea, I was beginning to climb the opposite shore, and I prepared to sing the song of Moses. But I have been disappointed, — those hopes have been blasted; those comforts have been wrested from me. I could not be so duped, even by the arch-enemy himself, as to be made to question the divine nature of them; but I have been made to believe (which, you will say, is being duped still more) that God gave them to me in derision, and took them away in vengeance. Such, however, is and has been my persuasion many a long day; and when I shall think on that subject more comfortably, or, as you will be inclined to tell me, more rationally and scripturally, I know not. In the mean time I embrace with alacrity every alleviation of my case, and with the more alacrity because whatsoever proves a relief of my distress is a cordial to Mrs. Unwin, whose sympathy with me through the whole of it has been such that, despair excepted, her burden has been as heavy as mine. Lady Hesketh, by her affectionate behavior, the cheerfulness of her conversation, and the constant sweetness of her temper, has cheered us both, and Mrs. Unwin not less than me. By her help we get change of air and of scene, though still resident at Olney; and by her means have intercourse with some families in this country, with whom, but for her, we could never have been acquainted. Her presence here would at any time, even in my happiest days, have been a comfort to me; but in the present day I am doubly sensible of its value. She leaves nothing unsaid, nothing undone, that she thinks will be conducive to our well-being; and so far as she is concerned, I have nothing to wish, but that I could believe her sent hither in mercy to myself, — then I should be thankful.

I understand that Mr. Bull is in town. If you should see him and happen to remember it, be so good as to tell him that we called at his door yesterday evening. All were well, but Mrs. B. and Mr. Greatheed were both abroad.

I am, my dear friend, with Mrs. Unwin's love to Mrs. N. and yourself, hers and yours, as ever.

LXVIII.

CONCERNING A REPROOF RECEIVED FROM MR. NEWTON.

To the Rev. William Unwin.

OLNEY, *September* 24, 1786.

MY DEAR WILLIAM, — . . . You have had your troubles, and we ours. This day three weeks your mother received a letter from Mr. Newton, which she has not yet answered, nor is likely to answer hereafter. It gave us both much concern, but her more than me, — I suppose because, my mind being necessarily occupied in my work, I had not so much leisure to browse upon the wormwood that it contained. The purport of it is a direct accusation of me, and of her an accusation implied, that we have both deviated into forbidden paths, and lead a life unbecoming the Gospel; that many of my friends in London are grieved, and the simple people of Olney astonished;

that he never so much doubted of my restoration to Christian privileges as now, — in short, that I converse too much with people of the world, and find too much pleasure in doing so. He concludes with putting your mother in mind that there is still an intercourse between London and Olney, — by which he means to insinuate that we cannot offend against the decorum that we are bound to observe, but the news of it will most certainly be conveyed to him. We do not at all doubt it; we never knew a lie hatched at Olney that waited long for a bearer; and though we do not wonder to find ourselves made the subjects of a false accusation in a place ever fruitful of such productions, we do and must wonder a little that he should listen to them with so much credulity. I say this because if he had heard only the truth, or had believed no more than the truth, he would not, I think, have found either me censurable or your mother. And that *she* should be suspected of irregularities is the more wonderful (for wonderful it would be at any rate), because she sent him not long before a letter conceived in such strains of piety and spirituality as ought to have convinced him that she at least was no wanderer. But what is the fact, and how do we spend our [time] in reality? What are the deeds for which we have been represented as thus criminal? Our present course of life differs in nothing from that which we have both held these thirteen years, — except that after great civilities shown us, and many advances made, on the part of the Throcks, we visit them; that we visit also at Gayhurst; that we have frequently taken airings with my cousin in her carriage; and that I have sometimes taken a walk with her on a Sunday evening, and sometimes by myself (which, however, your mother has never done), — these are the only novelties in our practice; and if by these procedures, so inoffensive in themselves, we yet give offence, offence must needs be given. God and our own consciences acquit us, and we acknowledge no other judges.

The two families with whom we have kicked up this astonishing intercourse are as harmless in their conversation and manners as can be found anywhere. And as to my poor cousin, the only crime that she is guilty of against the people of Olney is that she has fed the hungry, clothed the naked, and administered comfort to the sick, — except indeed that, by her great kindness, she has given us a little lift in point of condition and circumstances, and has thereby excited envy in some who have not the knack of rejoicing in the prosperity of others; and this I take to be the root of the matter.

My dear William, I do not know that I should have teased your nerves and spirits with this disagreeable theme, had not Mr. Newton talked of applying to you for particulars. He would have done it, he says, when he saw you last, but had not time. You are now qualified to inform him as minutely as we ourselves could of all our enormities! Adieu.

Our sincerest love to yourself and yours.

LXIX.

FEELINGS ON REMOVAL FROM OLNEY TO WESTON.

To the Rev. John Newton.

WESTON UNDERWOOD, *November* 17, 1786.

MY DEAR FRIEND, — My usual time of answering your letters having been unavoidably engrossed by occasions that would not be thrust aside, I have been obliged to postpone the payment of my debt for a whole week. Even now it is not without some difficulty that I discharge it, — which you will easily believe when I tell you that this is only the second day that has seen us inhabitants of our new abode. When God speaks to a chaos, it becomes a scene of order and harmony in a moment; but when his creatures have thrown one house into confusion by leaving it, and another by tumbling themselves and their goods into it, not less than many days' labor and contrivance is necessary to give them their proper places; and it belongs to furniture of all kinds, however convenient it may be in its place, to be a nuisance out of it. We find ourselves here in a comfortable dwelling, — such it is in itself; and my cousin, who has spared no expense in dressing it up for us, has made it a genteel one, — such, at least, it will be when its contents are a little harmonized. She left us on Tuesday; and on Wednesday, in the evening, Mrs. Unwin and I took possession. I could not help giving a last look to my old prison and its precincts, and — though I cannot easily account for it, having been miserable there so many years — felt something like a heartache when I took my last leave of a scene that certainly in itself had nothing to engage affection. But I recollected that I had once been happy there, and could not without tears in my eyes bid adieu to a place in which God had so often found me. The human mind is a great mystery, — mine, at least, appeared to me to be such upon this occasion. I found that I not only had a tenderness for that ruinous abode because it had once known me happy in the presence of God, but that even the distress I had suffered for so long a time on account of his absence had endeared it to me as much. I was weary of every object, had long wished for a change, yet could not take leave without a pang at parting. What consequences are to attend our removal God only knows. I know well that it is not in situation to effect a cure of melancholy like mine. The change, however, has been entirely a providential one; for much as I wished it, I never uttered that wish except to Mrs. Unwin. When I learned that the house was to be let, and had seen it, I had a strong desire that Lady Hesketh should take it for herself, if she should happen to like the country. That desire, indeed, is not exactly fulfilled, and yet, upon the whole, is exceeded. We are the tenants; but she assures us that we shall often have her for a guest; and here is room enough for us all. You, I hope, my dear friend, and Mrs. Newton will want no assurances to convince you that you will always be received here with the sincerest welcome. 'More welcome than you have been you cannot be; but better accommodated you may and will be.

I have not proceeded thus far without many interruptions, and though my paper is small, shall be obliged to make my letter still smaller. Our own removal is, I believe, the only news of Olney. Concerning this you will hear much, and much I doubt not that will have no truth in it. It is already reported there, and has been indeed for some time, that I am turned Papist. You will know how to treat a lie like this, which proves nothing but the malignity of its author; but other tales you may possibly hear that will not so readily refute themselves. This, however, I trust you will always find true: that neither Mrs. Unwin nor myself shall have so conducted ourselves in our new neighborhood as that you shall have any occasion to be grieved on our account.

Mr. Unwin has been ill of a fever at Winchester, but by a letter from Mr. Thornton we learn that he is recovering, and hopes soon to travel. His Mrs. Unwin has joined him at that place.

Adieu, my dear friend. Mrs. Unwin's affectionate remembrances and mine conclude me ever yours.

LXX.

COMFORTS OF THE NEW ABODE.

To Lady Hesketh.

WESTON LODGE, *November* 26, 1786.

IT is my birthday, my beloved cousin, and I determine to employ a part of it, that it may not be destitute of festivity, in writing to you. The dark, thick fog that has obscured it would have been a burden to me at Olney, but here I have hardly attended to it. The neatness and snugness of our abode compensate all the dreariness of the season; and whether the ways are wet or dry, our house at least is always warm and commodious. Oh for you, my cousin, to partake these comforts with us! I will not begin already to tease you upon that subject; but Mrs. Unwin remembers to have heard from your own lips that you hate London in the spring. Perhaps, therefore, by that time you may be glad to escape from a scene which will be every day growing more disagreeable, that you may enjoy the comforts of the lodge. You well know that the best house has a desolate appearance unfurnished. This house accordingly, since it has been occupied by us and our *meubles*, is as much superior to what it was when you saw it as you can imagine. The parlor is even elegant. When I say that the parlor is elegant, I do not mean to insinuate that the study is not so. It is neat, warm, and silent, and a much better study than I deserve if I do not produce in it an incomparable translation of Homer. I think every day of those lines of Milton, and congratulate myself on having obtained before I am quite superannuated what he seems not to have hoped for sooner, —

> "And may at length my weary age
> Find out the peaceful hermitage!"

For if it is not an hermitage, at least it is a much better thing; and you must always understand, my dear, that when poets talk of cottages, hermitages, and such like things, they mean a house with six sashes in front, two comfortable parlors, a smart staircase, and three bedchambers of convenient dimensions, — in short, exactly such a house as this.

The Throckmortons continue the most obliging neighbors in the world. One morning last week they both went with me to the cliff, — a scene, my dear, in which you would delight beyond measure, but which you cannot visit except in the spring or autumn. The heat of summer and the clinging dirt of winter would destroy you. What is called the "cliff" is no cliff, nor at all like one, but a beautiful terrace, sloping gently down to the Ouse, and from the brow of which, though not lofty, you have a view of such a valley as makes that which you see from the hills near Olney, and which I have had the honor to celebrate, — an affair of no consideration.[1]

Wintry as the weather is, do not suspect that it confines me. I ramble daily, and every day change my ramble. Wherever I go I find short grass under my feet, and when I have travelled perhaps five

[1] The Task, book i.

miles, come home with shoes not at all too dirty for a drawing-room. I was pacing yesterday under the elms that surround the field in which stands the great alcove, when, lifting my eyes, I saw two black genteel figures bolt through a hedge into the path where I was walking. You guess already who they were, and that they could be nobody but our neighbors. They had seen me from a hill at a distance, and had traversed a great turnip-field to get at me. You see therefore, my dear, that I am in some request, — alas! in too much request with some people. The verses of Cadwallader have found me at last.

I am charmed with your account of our little cousin[1] at Kensington. If the world does not spoil him hereafter, he will be a valuable man.

Good night, and may God bless thee!

LXXI.

ON THE DEATH OF REV. WILLIAM UNWIN.

To Lady Hesketh.

THE LODGE, *December* 4, 1786.

I SENT you, my dear, a melancholy letter, and I do not know that I shall now send you one very unlike it. Not that anything occurs in consequence of our late loss more afflictive than was to be expected, but the mind does not perfectly recover its tone after a shock like that which has been felt

[1] Lord Cowper.

so lately. This I observe, that though my experience has long since taught me that this is a world of shadows, and that it is the more prudent, as well as the more Christian, course to possess the comforts that we find in it as if we possessed them not, it is no easy matter to reduce this doctrine into practice. We forget that that God who gave them may, when he pleases, take them away, and that perhaps it may please him to take them at a time when we least expect, or are least disposed to part from them. Thus it has happened in the present case. There never was a moment in Unwin's life when there seemed to be more urgent want of him than the moment in which he died. He had attained to an age when, if they are at any time useful, men become useful to their families, their friends, and the world. His parish began to feel and to be sensible of the advantages of his ministry. The clergy around him were many of them awed by his example. His children were thriving under his own tuition and management, and his eldest boy is likely to feel his loss severely, being by his years in some respect qualified to understand the value of such a parent, — by his literary proficiency too clever for a schoolboy, and too young at the same time for the university. The removal of a man in the prime of life of such a character, and with such connections, seems to make a void in society that can never be filled. God seemed to have made him just what he was that he might be a blessing to others, and when the influence of his character and abilities began to be felt, removed him. These are mysteries, my dear, that we cannot contemplate without astonishment, but which will nevertheless be explained hereafter, and must in the mean time be revered in silence. It is well for his mother that she has spent her life in the practice of an habitual acquiescence in the dispensations of Providence, else I know that this stroke would have been heavier, after all that she has suffered upon another account, than she could have borne. She derives, as she well may, great consolation from the thought that he lived the life and died the death of a Christian. The consequence is, if possible, more unavoidable than the most mathematical conclusion that therefore he is happy. So farewell, my friend Unwin! the first man for whom I conceived a friendship after my removal from St. Alban's, and for whom I cannot but still continue to feel a friendship, though I shall see thee with these eyes no more!

LXXII.

HIS RECENT ILLNESS — DREAMS — FIRST ACQUAINTANCE WITH MR. ROSE.

To Lady Hesketh.

THE LODGE, *January* 18, 1787.

I HAVE been so much indisposed with the fever that I told you had seized me, my nights during the whole week may be said to have been almost sleepless. The consequence has been that except about thirty lines at the conclusion of the thirteenth book,

I have been forced to abandon Homer entirely. This was a sensible mortification to me, as you may suppose, and felt the more because, my spirits of course failing with my strength, I seemed to have peculiar need of my old amusement. It seemed hard, therefore, to be forced to resign it just when I wanted it most. But Homer's battles cannot be fought by a man who does not sleep well, and who has not some little degree of animation in the daytime. Last night, however, quite contrary to my expectations, the fever left me entirely, and I slept quietly, soundly, and long. If it please God that it return not, I shall soon find myself in a condition to proceed. I walk constantly, that is to say, Mrs. Unwin and I together; for at these times I keep her continually employed, and never suffer her to be absent from me many minutes. She gives me all her time and all her attention, and forgets that there is another object in the world.

Mrs. Carter thinks on the subject of dreams as everybody else does; that is to say, according to her own experience. She has had no extraordinary ones, and therefore accounts them only the ordinary operations of the fancy. Mine are of a texture that will not suffer me to ascribe them to so inadequate a cause, or to any cause but the operation of an exterior agency. I have a mind, my dear (and to you I will venture to boast of it), as free from superstition as any man living; neither do I give heed to dreams in general as predictive, though particular dreams I believe to be so. Some very sensible persons, and I suppose Mrs. Carter among them, will acknowledge that in old times God spoke by dreams, but affirm with much boldness that he has since ceased to do so. If you ask them why? they answer, because he has now revealed his will in the Scripture, and there is no longer any need that he should instruct or admonish us by dreams. I grant that with respect to doctrines and precepts he has left us in want of nothing; but has he thereby precluded himself in any of the operations of his Providence? Surely not. It is perfectly a different consideration; and the same need that there ever was of his interference in this way, there is still, and ever must be, while man continues blind and fallible, and a creature beset with dangers which he can neither foresee nor obviate. His operations however of this kind are, I allow, very rare; and as to the generality of dreams, they are made of such stuff, and are in themselves so insignificant, that though I believe them all to be the manufacture of others, not our own, I account it not a farthing-matter who manufactures them. So much for dreams!

My fever is not yet gone, but sometimes seems to leave me. It is altogether of the nervous kind, and attended now and then with much dejection.

A young gentleman called here yesterday, who came six miles out of his way to see me. He was on a journey to London from Glasgow, having just left the university there. He came, I suppose, partly to satisfy his own curiosity, but chiefly, as it seemed, to bring me the thanks of some of the Scotch professors for my two volumes. His name is Rose, an Englishman. Your spirits being good, you will derive more pleasure from this incident than I can at present, therefore I send it.

Adieu, very affectionately.[1]

LXXIII.

THANKS FOR A COPY OF BURNS.

To Samuel Rose, Esq.

WESTON, *July* 24, 1787.

DEAR SIR, — This is the first time I have written these six months, and nothing but the constraint of obligation could induce me to write now. I cannot be so wanting to myself as not to endeavor at least to thank you both for the visits with which you have favored me, and the poems that you sent me; in my present state of mind I taste nothing, nevertheless I read, partly from habit, and partly because it is the only thing that I am capable of.

I have therefore read Burns's poems, and have read them twice; and though they be written in a language that is new to me, and many of them on subjects much inferior to the author's ability, I think them on the whole a very extraordinary production. He is, I believe, the only poet these kingdoms have produced in the lower rank of life since Shakespeare

[1] These were the last lines that Cowper wrote before his malady returned upon him with full force. There is no other account of it than the little which is said in his own letters after his recovery.

(I should rather say since Prior) who need not be indebted for any part of his praise to a charitable consideration of his origin, and the disadvantages under which he has labored. It will be pity if he should not hereafter divest himself of barbarism, and content himself with writing pure English, in which he appears perfectly qualified to excel. He who can command admiration, dishonors himself if he aims no higher than to raise a laugh.

I am, dear sir, with my best wishes for your prosperity, and with Mrs. Unwin's respects,

Your obliged and affectionate humble servant.

LXXIV.

ARRIVAL OF A NEW-VICAR AT OLNEY. — A NEW CORRESPONDENT.

To the Rev. John Newton.

March 3, 1788.

MY DEAR FRIEND, — I had not, as you may imagine, read more than two or three lines of the inclosed, before I perceived that I had accidentally come to the possession of another man's property, who, by the same misadventure, has doubtless occupied mine. I accordingly folded it again the moment after having opened it, and now return it.

The bells of Olney both last night and this morning have announced the arrival of Mr. Bean. I understand that he is now come with his family. It will not be long, therefore, before we shall be acquainted. I rather wish than hope that he may find himself comfortably situated; but the parishioners' admiration of Mr. Canniford, whatever the bells may say, is no good omen. It is hardly to be expected that the same people should admire both. The parishioners of Ran'stone have been suitors to Mr. Finch that he would appoint that gentleman his curate, to which suit of theirs Mr. Finch has graciously condescended, and he is gone to reside among them.

I have lately been engaged in a correspondence with a lady whom I never saw; she lives at Pertenhall, near Kimbolton, and is the wife of a Dr. King, who has the living. She is, I understand, very happy in her husband, who for that reason, I should suppose, is at least no enemy to the Gospel, for she is evidently herself a Christian, and a very gracious one. I would that she had you for a correspondent rather than me. One letter from you would do her more good than a ream of mine. But so it is; and since I cannot depute my office to you, and am bound by all sorts of considerations to answer her this evening, I must necessarily quit you, that I may have time to do it.

LXXV.

SONG ON THE SLAVE-TRADE. — HANNAH MORE.

To Lady Hesketh.

THE LODGE, *March* 31, 1788.

MY DEAREST COUSIN, — Mrs. Throckmorton has promised to write to me. I beg that as often as you shall see her you will give her a smart pinch and say, " Have you written to my cousin? " I build all my hopes of her performance on this expedient, and for so doing these my letters, not patent, shall be your sufficient warrant. You are thus to give her the question till she shall answer " Yes."

I have written one more song, and sent it; it is called the " Morning Dream," and may be sung to the tune of " Tweed-Side," or any other tune that will suit it, for I am not nice on that subject. I would have copied it for you had I not almost filled my sheet without it; but now, my dear, you must stay till the sweet sirens of London shall bring it to you, or if that happy day should never arrive, I hereby acknowledge myself your debtor to that amount. I shall now probably cease to sing of tortured negroes, — a theme which never pleased me, but which, in the hope of doing them some little service, I was not unwilling to handle.

If anything could have raised Miss More to a higher place in my opinion than she possessed before, it could only be your information that, after all, she, and not Mr. Wilberforce, is author of that volume.[1] How comes it to pass that she, being a woman, writes with a force and energy and a correctness hitherto arrogated by the men, and not very frequently displayed even by the men themselves?   Adieu.

LXXVI.

ON THE LOSS OF HIS LIBRARY. — PRINTS OF CRAZY KATE AND THE LACEMAKER.

To Joseph Hill, Esq.

WESTON, *May* 8, 1788.

ALAS, my library! I must now give it up for a lost thing forever. The only consolation belonging to the circumstance is, or seems to be, that no such loss did ever befall any other man, or can ever befall me again. As far as books are concerned I am
Totus teres atque rotundus,
and may set fortune at defiance. The books which had been my father's had most of them his arms on the inside cover, but the rest no mark, neither his name nor mine. I could mourn for them like Sancho for his Dapple, but it would avail me nothing.

You will oblige me much by sending me "Crazy Kate." A gentleman last winter promised me both her and the "Lacemaker;" but he went to London,

[1] The Manners of the Great.

— that place in which, as in the grave, "all things are forgotten," — and I have never seen either of them.[1]

I begin to find some prospect of a conclusion of the Iliad, at least, now opening upon me, having reached the eighteenth book. Your letter found me yesterday in the very fact of dispersing the whole host of Troy by the voice only of Achilles. There is nothing extravagant in the idea, for you have witnessed a similar effect attending even such a voice as mine at midnight from a garret window, on the dogs of a whole parish, whom I have put to flight in a moment.

LXXVII.

THANKS FOR THE PRINTS. — ON THE NINETEENTH BOOK OF THE ILIAD.

To Joseph Hill, Esq.

May 24, 1788.

MY DEAR FRIEND, — For two excellent prints I return you my sincere acknowledgments. I cannot say that poor Kate resembles much the original, who was neither so young nor so handsome as the pencil has represented her; but she was a figure well suited to the account given of her in "The Task," and has a face exceedingly expressive of despairing melancholy. The lacemaker is

[1] He alludes to engravings of these two characters from "The Task," which had been made and become popular.

accidentally a good likeness of a young woman once our neighbor, who was hardly less handsome than the picture twenty years ago; but the loss of one husband and the acquisition of another have since that time impaired her much; yet she might still be supposed to have sat to the artist.[1]

We dined yesterday with your friend and mine, the most companionable and domestic Mr. C.[2] The whole kingdom can hardly furnish a spectacle more pleasing to a man who has a taste for true happiness than himself, Mrs. C., and their multitudinous family. Seven long miles are interposed between us, or perhaps I should oftener have an opportunity of declaiming on this subject.

I am now in the nineteenth book of the Iliad, and on the point of displaying such feats of heroism performed by Achilles as make all other achievements trivial. I may well exclaim, "Oh, for a muse of fire!" especially having not only a great host to cope with, but a great river also; much, however, may be done when Homer leads the way. I should not have chosen to have been the original author of such a business, even though all the Nine had stood at my elbow. Time has wonderful effects. We admire that in an ancient for which we should send a modern bard to Bedlam.

I saw at Mr. C.'s a great curiosity, — an antique bust of Paris in Parian marble. You will conclude that it interested me exceedingly. I pleased myself with supposing that it once stood in Helen's cham-

---

[1] Both characters were portraits drawn from real life.
[2] Mr. Chester of Chichely, near Newport-Pagnel.

ber. It was in fact brought from the Levant, and though not well mended (for it had suffered much by time), is an admirable performance.

LXXVIII.

ANTICIPATING A VISIT — THURLOW. — BEAU AND THE WATER-LILY.

To Lady Hesketh.

THE LODGE, *June* 27, 1788.

FOR the sake of a longer visit, my dearest coz, I can be well content to wait. The country — this country, at least — is pleasant at all times; and when winter is come, or near at hand, we shall have the better chance of being snug. I know your passion for retirement indeed, or for what we call *deedy* retirement; and the F——s intending to return to Bath with their mother when her visit at the Hall is over, you will then find here exactly the retirement in question. I have made in the orchard the best winter-walk in all the parish, sheltered from the east and from the northeast, and open to the sun, except at his rising, all the day. Then we will have Homer and Don Quixote; and then we will have saunter and chat, and one laugh more before we die. Our orchard is alive with creatures of all kinds; poultry of every denomination swarms in it, and pigs the drollest in the world.

I rejoice that we have a cousin Charles also, as well as a cousin Henry, who has had the address to win the good-likings of the Chancellor. May he fare the better for it! As to myself, I have long since ceased to have any expectations from that quarter. Yet, if he were indeed mortified as you say (and no doubt you have particular reasons for thinking so), and repented to that degree of his hasty exertions in favor of the present occupant (who can tell?), he wants neither means nor management, but can easily at some future period redress the evil, if he chooses to do it. But in the mean time life steals away, and shortly neither he will be in circumstances to do me a kindness, nor I to receive one at his hands. Let him make haste, therefore, or he will die a promise in my debt which he will never be able to perform.[1] Your communications on this subject are as safe as you can wish them. We divulge nothing but what might appear in the magazine, nor that without great consideration.

I must tell you a feat of my dog Beau. Walking by the river side, I observed some water-lilies floating at a little distance from the bank. They are a large white flower, with an orange-colored eye, very beautiful. I had a desire to gather one, and having your long cane in my hand, by the help of it endeavored to bring one of them within my reach. But the attempt proved vain, and I walked forward. Beau had all the while observed me attentively. Returning soon after toward the same place, I observed him plunge into the river while I was about forty yards' distance from him; and when I had nearly

[1] An allusion to his youthful promise to make some provision for Cowper when he should become Lord Chancellor.

reached the spot he swam to land with a lily in his mouth, which he came and laid at my foot.[1]

Mr. Rose, whom I have mentioned to you as a visitor of mine for the first time soon after you left us, writes me word that he has seen my ballads against the slave-mongers, but not in print.[2] Where he met with them I know not. Mr. Bull begged hard for leave to print them at Newport-Pagnel, and I refused, thinking that it would be wrong to anticipate the nobility, gentry, and others at whose pressing instance I composed them, in their design to print them. But perhaps I need not have been so squeamish; for the opportunity to publish them in London seems now not only ripe, but rotten. I am well content. There is but one of them with which I am myself satisfied, though I have heard them all well spoken of. But there are very few things of my own composition that I can endure to read when they have been written a month, though at first they seem to me to be all perfection.

Mrs. Unwin, who has been much the happier since the time of your return hither has been in some sort settled, begs me to make her kindest remembrance.

Yours, my dear, most truly.

[1] This incident also forms the subject of one of his poems.
[2] These were never printed as ballads, but were included later with his poems.

LXXIX.

THE LIME-WALK. — FIVE HUNDRED CELEBRATED LIVING AUTHORS; HIS OWN RANK AMONG THEM.

To Lady Hesketh.

THE LODGE, *July* 28, 1788.

IT is in vain that you tell me you have no talent at description, while in fact you describe better than anybody. You have given me a most complete idea of your mansion and its situation; and I doubt not that with your letter in my hand by way of map, could I be set down on the spot in a moment, I should find myself qualified to take my walks and my pastime in whatever quarter of your paradise it should please me the most to visit. We also, as you know, have scenes at Weston worthy of description; but because you know them well, I will only say that one of them has, within these few days, been much improved, — I mean the lime-walk. By the help of the axe and the wood-bill, which have of late been constantly employed in cutting out all straggling branches that intercepted the arch, Mr. Throckmorton has now defined it with such exactness that no cathedral in the world can show one of more magnificence or beauty. I bless myself that I live so near it; for were it distant several miles, it would be well worth while to visit it, merely as an object of taste, not to mention the refreshment of such a gloom both to the eyes and the spirits. And these are the things which our modern improvers of parks and pleasure-grounds have displaced without mercy, because, forsooth, they are rectilinear! It is a wonder they do not quarrel with the sunbeams for the same reason.

Have you seen the account of Five hundred celebrated authors now living? I am one of them, but stand charged with the high crime and misdemeanor of totally neglecting method, — an accusation which, if the gentleman would take the pains to read me, he would find sufficiently refuted. I am conscious at least of having labored much in the arrangement of my matter, and of having given to the several parts of my book of "The Task," as well as to each poem in the first volume, that sort of slight connection which poetry demands; for in poetry (except professedly of the didactic kind) a logical precision would be stiff, pedantic, and ridiculous. But there is no pleasing some critics; the comfort is that I am contented whether they be pleased or not. At the same time, to my honor be it spoken, the chronicler of us five hundred prodigies bestows on me, for aught I know, more commendations than on any other of my confraternity. May he live to write the histories of as many thousand poets, and find me the very best among them! Amen!

I join with you, my dearest coz, in wishing that I owned the fee-simple of all the beautiful scenes around you; but such emoluments were never designed for poets. Am I not happier than ever poet was in having thee for my cousin, and in the expectation of thy arrival here whenever Strawberry Hill [1] shall lose thee? Ever thine.

[1] Lady Hesketh was the guest of Horace Walpole at Strawberry Hill at this time.

LXXX.

COMPLETION OF THE ILIAD, AND BEGINNING OF THE ODYSSEY.

To Samuel Rose, Esq.

WESTON, *September 25, 1788.*

MY DEAR FRIEND:

Say what is the thing by my riddle design'd
Which you carried to London, and yet left behind?

I expect your answer, and without a fee. The half hour next before breakfast I devote to you. The moment Mrs. Unwin arrives in the study, be what I have written much or little, I shall make my bow and take leave. If you live to be a judge, as if I augur right you will, I shall expect to hear of a walking circuit.

I was shocked at what you tell me of ———. Superior talents, it seems, give no security for propriety of conduct; on the contrary, having a natural tendency to nourish pride, they often betray the possessor into such mistakes as men more moderately gifted never commit. Ability, therefore, is not wisdom, and an ounce of grace is a better guard against gross absurdity than the brightest talents in the world.

I rejoice that you are prepared for transcript work: here will be plenty for you. The day on which you shall receive this I beg you will remember to drink one glass at least to the success of the Iliad, which I finished the day before yesterday, and yesterday began the Odyssey. It will be some time before I shall perceive myself travelling in another road; the objects around me are at present so much the same: Olympus and a council of gods meet me at my first entrance. To tell you the truth, I am weary of heroes and deities, and, with reverence be it spoken, shall be glad, for variety's sake, to exchange their company for that of a Cyclops.

Weston has not been without its tragedies since you left us. Mr. Throckmorton's piping bullfinch has been eaten by a rat, and the villain left nothing but poor Bully's beak behind him. It will be a wonder if this event does not at some convenient time employ my versifying passion. Did ever fair lady, from the Lesbia of Catullus to the present day, lose her bird and find no poet to commemorate the loss?

LXXXI.

ACCOUNT OF HIS OCCUPATIONS BEFORE HE UNDERTOOK POETRY.

To Mrs. King.

WESTON UNDERWOOD, *October* 11, 1788.

MY DEAR MADAM, — You are perfectly secure from all danger of being overwhelmed with presents from me. It is not much that a poet can possibly have it in his power to give. When he has presented his own works, he may be supposed to have exhausted all means of donation. They are his only superfluity. There was a time, but that time was before I commenced writer for the press, when I amused myself in a way somewhat similar to yours, allowing, I mean, for the difference between masculine and female operations. The scissors and the needle are your chief implements; mine were the chisel and the saw. In those days you might have been in some danger of too plentiful a return for your favors. Tables, such as they were, and joint stools, such as never were, might have travelled to Pertenhall in most inconvenient abundance. But I have long since discontinued this practice, and many others which I found it necessary to adopt, that I might escape the worst of all evils, both in itself and in its consequences, — an idle life. Many arts I have exercised with this view, for which Nature never designed me; though among them were some in which I arrived at considerable proficiency, by mere dint of the most heroic perseverance. There is not a 'squire in all this country who can boast of having made better squirrel-houses, hutches for rabbits, or bird-cages, than myself; and in the article of cabbage-nets I had no superior. I even had the hardiness to take in hand the pencil, and studied a whole year the art of drawing. Many figures were the fruit of my labors, which had at least the merit of being unparalleled by any production either of art or nature. But before the year was ended, I had occasion to wonder at the progress that may be made, in despite of natural deficiency, by dint alone of practice; for I actually produced three landscapes which a lady thought worthy to be framed and glazed. I then judged it high time to exchange this occupation for another, lest, by any subsequent productions of inferior merit, I should forfeit the honor I had so fortunately acquired. But gardening was, of all employments, that in which I succeeded best, — though even in this I did not suddenly attain perfection. I began with lettuces and cauliflowers; from them I proceeded to cucumbers; next, to melons. I then purchased an orange-tree, to which, in due time, I added two or three myrtles. These served me day and night with employment during a whole severe winter. To defend them from the frost, in a situation that exposed them to its severity, cost me much ingenuity and much attendance. I contrived to give them a fire heat; and have waded night after night through the snow, with the bellows under my arm, just before going to bed, to give the latest possible puff to the embers, lest the frost should seize them before morning. Very minute beginnings have sometimes important consequences. From nursing two or three little evergreens, I became ambitious of a greenhouse, and accordingly built one, which, verse excepted, afforded me amusement for a longer time than any expedient of all the many to which I have fled for refuge from the misery of having nothing to do. When I left Olney for Weston, I could no longer have a greenhouse of my own, but in a neighbor's garden I find a better, of which the sole management is consigned to me.

I had need take care, when I begin a letter, that the subject with which I set off be of some importance; for before I can exhaust it, be it what it may, I have generally filled my paper. But self is a subject inexhaustible, which is the reason that though I have said little or nothing, I am afraid, worth your hearing, I have only room to add that I am, my dear madam,

Most truly yours.

Mrs. Unwin bids me present her best compliments, and say how much she shall be obliged to you for the receipt to make that most excellent cake which came hither in its native pan. There is no production of yours that will not always be most welcome at Weston.

LXXXII.

CHANGES, ESPECIALLY AT THE PLACE OF HIS BIRTH.

To Mrs. King.

WESTON UNDERWOOD, *December* 6, 1788.

MY DEAR MADAM, — It must, if you please, be a point agreed between us that we will not make punctuality in writing the test of our regard for each other, lest we should incur the danger of pronouncing and suffering by an unjust sentence, and this mutually. I have told you, I believe, that the half hour before breakfast is my only letter-writing opportunity. In summer I rise rather early, and consequently at that season can find more time for scribbling than at present. If I enter my study now before nine, I find all at sixes and sevens; for servants will take, in part at least, the liberty claimed by their masters. That you may not suppose us all sluggards alike, it is necessary, however, that I should add a word or two on this subject in justification of Mrs. Unwin, who, because the days are too short for the important concerns of knitting stockings and mending them, rises generally by candle-light, — a practice so much in the style of all the ladies of antiquity who were good for anything that it is impossible not to applaud it.

Mrs. Battison[1] being dead, I began to fear that you would have no more calls to Bedford; but the marriage, so near at hand, of the young lady you mention with a gentleman of that place, gives me hope again that you may occasionally approach us as heretofore, and that on some of those occasions you will perhaps find your way to Weston. The deaths of some, and the marriages of others, make a new world of it every thirty years. Within that space of time the majority are displaced and a new generation has succeeded. Here and there one is permitted to stay a little longer, that there may not be wanting a few grave dons like myself to make the observation. This thought struck me very forcibly the other day on reading a paper called the "County Chronicle," which came hither in the package of some books from London. It contained

[1] A relative of Mrs. King's whom she had been accustomed to visit at Bedford.

news from Hertfordshire, and informed me, among other things, that at Great Berkhampstead, the place of my birth, there is hardly a family left of all those with whom, in my earlier days, I was so familiar. The houses, no doubt, remain, but the inhabitants are only to be found now by their gravestones; and it is certain that I might pass through a town, in which I was once a sort of principal figure, unknowing and unknown. They are happy who have not taken up their rest in a world fluctuating as the sea, and passing away with the rapidity of a river. I wish from my heart that yourself and Mr. King may long continue, as you have already long continued, exceptions from the general truth of this remark. You doubtless married early, and the thirty-six years elapsed may have yet other years to succeed them; I do not forget that your relation Mrs. Battison lived to the age of eighty-six. I am glad of her longevity, because it seems to afford some assurances of yours, and I hope to know you better yet before you die.

Should you again dream of an interview with me, I hope you will have the precaution to shut all doors and windows, that no such impertinents as those you mention may intrude a second time. It is hard that people who never meet awake, cannot come together even in sleep without disturbance. We might, I think, be ourselves untroubled at a time when we are so incapable of giving trouble to others, even had we the inclination.

I have never seen "The Observer," but am pleased with being handsomely spoken of by an old schoolfellow. Cumberland [1] and I boarded together in the same house at Westminster. He was at that time clever, and I suppose has given proof sufficient to the world that he is still clever; but of all that he has written, it has never fallen in my way to read a syllable, except perhaps in a magazine or review, — the sole sources at present of all my intelligence. Addison speaks of persons who grow dumb in the study of eloquence, and I have actually studied Homer till I am become a mere ignoramus in every other province of literature.

An almost general cessation of egg-laying among the hens has made it impossible for Mrs. Unwin to enterprise a cake. She however returns you a thousand thanks for the receipt; and being now furnished with the necessary ingredients, will begin directly. My letter-writing time is spent, and I must now to Homer. With my best respects to Mr. King, I remain, dear madam,

Most affectionately yours.

When I wrote last I told you, I believe, that Lady Hesketh was with us. She is with us now, making a cheerful winter for us at Weston. The acquisition of a new friend, and, at a late day, the recovery of the friend of our youth, are two of the chief comforts of which this life is susceptible.

[1] Author of a series of essays called "The Observer."

LXXXIII.

MRS. UNWIN'S ACCIDENT.—THE KING'S ILLNESS.

To Mrs. King.

WESTON, *January* 29, 1789.

MY DEAR MADAM, — This morning I said to Mrs. Unwin: "I must write to Mrs. King; her long silence alarms me: something has happened." These words of mine proved only a prelude to the arrival of your messenger with his most welcome charge, for which I return you my sincerest thanks. You have sent me the very things I wanted, and which I should have continued to want had not you sent them. As often as the wine is set on the table I have said to myself, "This is all very well; but I have no bottle-stands." And myself as often replied, "No matter; you can make shift without them." Thus I and myself have conferred together many a day; and you, as if you had been privy to the conference, have kindly supplied the deficiency, and put an end to the debate forever.

When your messenger arrived I was beginning to dress for dinner, being engaged to dine with my neighbor Mr. Throckmorton, from whose house I am just returned, and snatch a few moments before supper to tell you how much I am obliged to you. You will not, therefore, find me very prolix at present; but it shall not be long before you shall hear further from me. Your honest old neighbor sleeps under our roof, and will be gone in the morning before I shall have seen him.

I have more items than one by which to remember the late frost: it has cost me the bitterest uneasiness. Mrs. Unwin got a fall on the gravel-walk covered with ice, which has confined her to an upper chamber ever since. She neither broke nor dislocated any bones, but received such a contusion below the hip as crippled her completely. She now begins to recover, after having been helpless as a child for a whole fortnight, but so slowly at present that her amendment is even now almost imperceptible.

Engaged, however, as I am with my own private anxieties, I yet find leisure to interest myself not a little in the distresses of the royal family, especially in those of the Queen.[1] The Lord Chancellor called the other morning on Lord Stafford; entering the room, he threw his hat on the sofa at the fireside, and clasping his hands, said, "I have heard of distress, and I have read of it; but I never saw distress equal to that of the Queen." This I know from particular and certain authority.

My dear madam, I have not time to enlarge at present on this subject, or to touch any other. Once more, therefore, thanking you for your kindness, of which I am truly sensible, and thanking, too, Mr. King for the favor he has done me in subscribing to my Homer, and at the same time begging you to

[1] Because of the temporary insanity of the King, George III.

make my best compliments to him, I conclude myself, with Mrs. Unwin's acknowledgments of your most acceptable present to her,
Your obliged and affectionate.

LXXXIV.

ON HIS ABSORPTION IN HOMER.

To the Rev. Walter Bagot.

WESTON, *January* 29, 1789.

MY DEAR FRIEND, — I shall be a better, at least a more frequent, correspondent when I have done with Homer. I am not forgetful of any letters that I owe, and least of all forgetful of my debts in that way to you; on the contrary, I live in a continual state of self-reproach for not writing more punctually; but the old Grecian, whom I charge myself never to neglect, lest I should never finish him, has at present a voice that seems to drown all other demands, and many to which I could listen with more pleasure than even his *os rotundum*. I am now in the eleventh book of the Odyssey, conversing with the dead. Invoke the Muse in my behalf, that I may roll the stone of Sisyphus with some success. To do it as Homer has done it is, I suppose, in our verse and language, impossible; but I will hope not to labor altogether to as little purpose as Sisyphus himself did.

Though I meddle little with politics, and can find but little leisure to do so, the present state of things unavoidably engages a share of my attention. But as they say Archimedes, when Syracuse was taken, was found busied in the solution of a problem, so, come what may, I shall be found translating Homer.   Sincerely yours.

LXXXV.

DISSATISFACTION WITH HIS OWN WRITING. — UNCONSCIOUS PLAGIARISM.

To Samuel Rose, Esq.

THE LODGE, *May* 20, 1789.

MY DEAR SIR, — Finding myself, between twelve and one, at the end of the seventeenth book of the Odyssey, I give the interval between the present moment and the time of walking to you. If I write letters before I sit down to Homer, I feel my spirits too flat for poetry, and too flat for letter-writing if I address myself to Homer first; but the last I choose as the least evil, because my friends will pardon my dulness, but the public will not.

I had been some days uneasy on your account, when yours arrived. We should have rejoiced to have seen you, would your engagements have permitted; but in the autumn I hope, if not before, we shall have the pleasure to receive you. At what time we may expect Lady Hesketh, at present I know not, but imagine that at any time after the month of June you will be sure to find her with us, — which I mention knowing that to meet you will add a relish to all the pleasures she can find at Weston.

When I wrote those lines on the Queen's visit I thought I had performed well; but it belongs to me, as I have told you before, to dislike whatever I write when it has been written a month; the performance was therefore sinking in my esteem when your approbation of it, arriving in good time, buoyed it up again. It will now keep possession of the place it holds in my good opinion because it has been favored with yours; and a copy will certainly be at your service whenever you choose to have one.

Nothing is more certain than that when I wrote the line, —

> God made the country, and man made the town,

I had not the least recollection of that very similar one which you quote from Hawkins Browne. It convinces me that critics (and none more than Warton in his notes on Milton's minor poems) have often charged authors with borrowing what they drew from their own fund. Browne was an entertaining companion when he had drunk his bottle, but not before; this proved a snare to him, and he would sometimes drink too much; but I know not that he was chargeable with any other irregularities. He had those among his intimates who would not have been such had he been otherwise viciously inclined, — the Duncombes in particular, father and son, who were of unblemished morals.

LXXXVI.

STANZAS ON THE QUEEN'S VISIT TO LONDON PRESENTED TO HER MAJESTY.

To Mrs. King.

WESTON, *May* 30, 1789.

DEAREST MADAM, — Many thanks for your kind and valuable despatches, none of which, except your letter, I have yet had time to read; for true it is, and a sad truth too, that I was in bed when your messenger arrived. He waits only for my answer, for which reason I answer as speedily as I can.

I am glad if my poetical packet pleased you. Those stanzas on the Queen's visit were presented some time since, by Miss Goldsworthy, to the Princess Augusta, who has probably given them to the Queen; but of their reception I have heard nothing. I gratified myself by complimenting two sovereigns whom I love and honor; and that gratification will be my reward. It would, indeed, be unreasonable to expect that persons who keep a Laureate in constant pay, should have either praise or emolument to spare for every volunteer scribbler who may choose to make them his subject.

Mrs. Unwin, who is much obliged to you for your inquiries, is but little better since I wrote last. No person ever recovered more imperceptibly; yet certain it is that she does recover. I am persuaded myself that, though it was not suspected at the time, the thigh-bone was longitudinally fractured; and she is of my opinion. Much time is requisite to the restoration of a bone so injured, and nothing can be done to expedite the cure. My mother-in-law broke her leg-bone in the same manner, and was long a cripple. The only comfort in the present case is that had the bone been broken transversely, the consequences must probably have been mortal.

I will take the greatest care of the papers with which you have intrusted me, and will return them by the next opportunity. It is very unfortunate that the people of Bedford should choose to have the small-pox just at the season when it would be sure to prevent our meeting. God only knows, madam, when we shall meet, or whether at all in this world; but certain it is that, whether we meet or not,

I am most truly yours.

LXXXVII.

ON THE RECEIPT OF A HAMPER (IN THE MANNER OF HOMER).

To Samuel Rose, Esq.

WESTON, *October* 4, 1789.

MY DEAR FRIEND, — The hamper is come, and come safe; and the contents I can affirm on my own knowledge are excellent. It chanced that another hamper and box came by the same conveyance, all which I unpacked and expounded in the hall, my cousin sitting meantime on the stairs spectatress of the business. We diverted ourselves with imagining the manner in which Homer would have described the scene. Detailed in his circumstantial way, it would have furnished materials for a paragraph of considerable length in an Odyssey.

> The straw-stuff'd hamper with his ruthless steel
> He open'd, cutting sheer th' inserted cords,
> Which bound the lid and lip secure. Forth came
> The rustling package first, bright straw of wheat,
> Or oats, or barley; next a bottle green
> Throat-full, clear spirits the contents, distill'd
> Drop after drop odorous, by the art
> Of the fair mother of his friend — the Rose.

And so on. I should rejoice to be the hero of such a tale in the hands of Homer.

You will remember, I trust, that when the state of your health or spirits calls for rural walks and fresh air, you have always a retreat at Weston.

We are all well, all love you, down to the very dog, and shall be glad to hear that you have exchanged languor for alacrity, and the debility that you mention for indefatigable vigor.

Mr. Throckmorton has made me a handsome present, — Villoison's edition of the Iliad, elegantly bound by Edwards. If I live long enough, by the contributions of my friends I shall once more be possessed of a library.

Adieu.

LXXXVIII.

SUMMARY OF HIS PRESENT SITUATION.

To the Rev. John Newton.

December 1, 1789.

MY DEAR FRIEND, — On this fine first of December, under an uncloudy sky, and in a room full of sunshine, I address myself to the payment of a debt long in arrear, but never forgotten by me, however I may have seemed to forget it. I will not waste time in apologies. I have but one, and that one will suggest itself unmentioned. I will only add that you are the first to whom I write of several to whom I have not written many months, who all have claims upon me, and who I flatter myself are all grumbling at my silence. In your case perhaps I have been less anxious than in the case of some others, because if you have not heard from myself, you have heard from Mrs. Unwin. From her you have learned that I live, that I am as well as usual, and that I translate Homer, — three short items, but in which is comprised the whole detail of my present history. Thus I fared when you were here; thus I have fared ever since you were here; and thus, if it please God, I shall continue to fare for some time longer; for, though the work is done, it is not finished, — a riddle which you, who are a brother of the press, will solve easily. I have also been the less anxious because I have had frequent opportunities to hear of you, and have always heard that you are in good health and happy. Of Mrs. Newton, too, I have heard more favorable accounts of late, which have given us both the sincerest pleasure. Mrs. Unwin's case is at present my only subject of uneasiness that is not immediately personal and properly my own. She has almost constant headaches, almost a constant pain in her side which nobody understands, and her lameness within the last half year is very little amended. But her spirits are good because supported by comforts which depend not on the state of the body; and I do not know that, with all these pains, her looks are at all altered since we had the happiness to see you here, — unless perhaps they are altered a little for the better. I have thus given you as circumstantial an account of ourselves as I could, — the most interesting matter I verily believe with which I could have filled my paper, unless I could have made spiritual mercies to myself the subject. In my next perhaps I shall find leisure to bestow a few lines on what is doing in France and in the Austrian Netherlands, — though, to say the truth, I am much better qualified to write an essay on the siege of Troy than to descant on any of these modern revolutions. I question if in either of the countries just mentioned, full of bustle and tumult as they are, there be a single character whom Homer, were he living, would deign to make his hero. The populace are the heroes now; and the stuff of which gentlemen heroes are made seems to be all expended.

I will endeavor that my next letter shall not follow this so tardily as this has followed the last; and with our joint affectionate remembrances to yourself and Mrs. Newton, remain as ever,

> Sincerely yours.

LXXXIX.

FIRST APPEARANCE OF THE FRENCH REVOLUTION.

To Joseph Hill, Esq.

> WESTON, *December* 18, 1789.

MY DEAR FRIEND, — The present appears to me a wonderful period in the history of mankind. That nations so long contentedly slaves should on a sudden become enamoured of liberty, and understand as suddenly their own natural right to it, feeling themselves at the same time inspired with resolution to assert it, seems difficult to account for from natural causes. With respect to the final issue of all this, I can only say that if, having discovered the value of liberty, they should next discover the value of peace, and lastly the value of the word of God, they will be happier than they ever were since the rebellion of the first pair, and as happy as it is possible they should be in the present life.

> Most sincerely yours.

XC.

FOREBODINGS OF THE MONTH OF JANUARY.

To the Rev. John Newton.

February 5, 1790.

MY DEAR FRIEND, — Your kind letter deserved a speedier answer, but you know my excuse, which were I to repeat always, my letters would resemble the fag-end of a newspaper, where we always find the price of stocks detailed with little or no variation.

When January returns you have your feelings concerning me, and such as prove the faithfulness of your friendship. I have mine also concerning myself, but they are of a cast different from yours. Yours have a mixture of sympathy and tender solicitude which makes them, perhaps, not altogether unpleasant. Mine, on the contrary, are of an unmixed nature, and consist simply and merely of the most alarming apprehensions. Twice has that month returned upon me, accompanied by such horrors as I have no reason to suppose ever made part of the experience of any other man. I accordingly look forward to it and meet it with a dread not to be imagined. I number the nights as they pass, and in the morning bless myself that another night is gone and no harm has happened. This may argue, perhaps, some imbecility of mind, and no small degree of it; but it is natural, I believe, and so natural as to be necessary and unavoidable. I know that God is not governed by secondary causes in any of his operations, and that, on the contrary, they are all so many agents in his hand, which strike only when he bids them. I know, consequently, that one month is as dangerous to me as another, and that in the middle of summer at noonday and in the clear sunshine I am, in reality, unless guarded by him, as much exposed as when fast asleep at midnight and in midwinter. But we are not always the wiser for our knowledge, and I can no more avail myself of mine than if it were in the head of another man, and not in my own. I have heard of bodily aches and ails that have been particularly troublesome when the season returned in which the hurt that occasioned them was received. The mind, I believe (with my own, however, I am sure it is so), is liable to similar periodical affection. But February is come, January, my terror, is passed, and some shades of the gloom that attended his presence have passed with him. I look forward with a little cheerfulness to the buds and the leaves that will soon appear, and say to myself, till they turn yellow I will make myself easy. The year *will* go round, and January *will* approach. I *shall* tremble again, and I know it; but in the mean time I will be as comfortable as I can. Thus, in respect of peace of mind, such as it is that I enjoy, I subsist, as the poor are vulgarly said to do, from hand to mouth; and, of a Christian, such as you once knew me, am, by a strange transformation, become an Epicurean philosopher, bearing this motto on my mind, — *Quid sit futurum cras, fuge quærere.*

I have run on in a strain that the beginning of your letter suggested to me, with such impetuosity that I have not left myself opportunity to write more by the present post; and being unwilling that you should wait longer for what will be worth nothing when you get it, will only express the great pleasure we feel on hearing, as we did lately from Mr. Bull, that Mrs. Newton is so much better.

Mrs. Unwin has been very indifferent all the winter, harassed by continual headaches and want of sleep, the consequences of a nervous fever; but I hope she begins to recover.

With our best love to Mrs. Newton, not forgetting Miss Catlett, I remain, my dear friend,

Truly yours.

XCI.

ON RECEIVING A PRESENT OF HIS MOTHER'S PICTURE.

To Lady Hesketh.

THE LODGE, *February* 26, 1790.

You have set my heart at ease, my cousin, so far as you were yourself the object of its anxieties. What other troubles it feels can be cured by God alone. But you are never silent a week longer than usual without giving an opportunity to my imagination (ever fruitful in flowers of a sable hue) to tease me with them day and night. London is indeed a pestilent place, as you call it, and I would, with all my heart, that thou hadst less to do with it;

were you under the same roof with me, I should know you to be safe, and should never distress you with melancholy letters.

I feel myself well enough inclined to the measure you propose, and will show to your new acquaintance with all my heart a sample of my translation, but it shall not, if you please, be taken from the Odyssey. It is a poem of a gentler character than the Iliad, and as I propose to carry her by a *coup de main*, I shall employ Achilles, Agamemnon, and the two armies of Greece and Troy in my service. I will accordingly send you, in the box that I received from you last night, the two first books of the Iliad for that lady's perusal; to those I have given a third revisal; for them, therefore, I will be answerable, and am not afraid to stake the credit of my work upon *them* with her, or with any living wight, especially one who understands the original. I do not mean that even they are finished, for I shall examine and cross-examine them yet again, and so you may tell her; but I know that they will not disgrace me: whereas it is so long since I have looked at the Odyssey that I know nothing at all about it. They shall set sail from Olney on Monday morning in the Diligence, and will reach you, I hope, in the evening. As soon as she has done with them, I shall be glad to have them again, for the time draws near when I shall want to give them the last touch.

I am delighted with Mrs. Bodham's[1] kindness

---

[1] Mrs. Bodham had been a favorite cousin of Cowper's in their childhood. During twenty-seven years he had held no

in giving me the only picture of my own mother that is to be found, I suppose, in all the world. I had rather possess it than the richest jewel in the British crown, for I loved her with an affection that her death, fifty-two years since, has not in the least abated. I remember her too, young as I was when she died, well enough to know that it is a very exact resemblance of her, and, as such, it is to me invaluable. Everybody loved her, and with an amiable character so impressed upon all her features, everybody was sure to do so.

I have a very affectionate and a very clever letter from Johnson, who promises me the transcript of the books intrusted to him in a few days. I have a great love for that young man; he has some drops of the same stream in his veins that once animated the original of that dear picture.

intercourse with his maternal relations, and had entirely disappeared from their knowledge until he became known to the public. John Johnson, grandson of his mother's brother, Roger Donne, then sought him out at Weston. A report of his visit to his aunt, Mrs. Bodham, led her to write to Cowper, enclosing a picture of his mother.

XCII.

ACKNOWLEDGING THE RECEIPT OF HIS MOTHER'S PICTURE.

To Mrs. Bodham.

WESTON, *February* 27, 1790.

MY DEAREST ROSE,[1] — Whom I thought withered and fallen from the stalk, but whom I find still alive, nothing could give me greater pleasure than to know it, and to learn it from yourself. I loved you dearly when you were a child, and love you not a jot the less for having ceased to be so. Every creature that bears any affinity to my mother is dear to me, and you, the daughter of her brother, are but one remove distant from her; I love you, therefore, and love you much, both for her sake and for your own. The world could not have furnished you with a present so acceptable to me as the picture which you have so kindly sent me. I received it the night before last, and viewed it with a trepidation of nerves and spirits somewhat akin to what I should have felt had the dear original presented herself to my embraces. I kissed it, and hung it where it is the last object that I see at night, and, of course, the first on which I open my eyes in the morning. She died when I completed my sixth year; yet I remember her well, and am an ocular witness of the great fidelity of the copy. I remem-

---

[1] Cowper's pet name for his cousin. Mrs. Bodham's Christian name was Ann.

ber, too, a multitude of the maternal tendernesses which I received from her, and which have endeared her memory to me beyond expression. There is in me, I believe, more of the Donne[1] than of the Cowper; and though I love all of both names, and have a thousand reasons to love those of my own name, yet I feel the bond of nature draw me vehemently to your side. I was thought in the days of my childhood much to resemble my mother; and in my natural temper, of which, at the age of fifty-eight, I must be supposed to be a competent judge, can trace both her and my late uncle, your father. Somewhat of his irritability, and a little, I would hope, both of his and of her ——, I know not what to call it, without seeming to praise myself, which is not my intention, but speaking to *you*, I will even speak out and say, *good nature*. Add to all this, I deal much in poetry, as did our venerable ancestor, the Dean of St. Paul's, and I think I shall have proved myself a Donne at all points. The truth is, that whatever I am, I love you all.

I account it a happy event that brought the dear boy, your nephew, to my knowledge, and that, breaking through all the restraints which his natural bashfulness imposed on him, he determined to find me out. He is amiable to a degree that I have seldom seen, and I often long with impatience to see him again.

My dearest cousin, what shall I say in answer to your affectionate invitation? I *must* say this: I cannot come now, nor soon, and I wish with all my heart I

---

[1] The family name of Cowper's mother.

could. But I will tell you what may be done, perhaps, and it will answer to us just as well, — you and Mr. Bodham can come to Weston; can you not? The summer is at hand, there are roads and wheels to bring you, and you are neither of you translating Homer. I am crazed that I cannot ask you all together, for want of house-room; but for Mr. Bodham and yourself we have good room; and equally good for any third, in the shape of a Donne, whether named Hewitt, Bodham, Balls, or Johnson, or by whatever name distinguished. Mrs. Hewitt has particular claims upon me; she was my playfellow at Berkhamstead, and has a share in my warmest affections. Pray tell her so! Neither do I at all forget my cousin Harriet. She and I have been many a time merry at Catfield, and have made the parsonage ring with laughter. Give my love to her. Assure yourself, my dearest cousin, that I shall receive you as if you were my sister, and Mrs. Unwin is, for my sake, prepared to do the same. When she has seen you, she will love you for your own.

I am much obliged to Mr. Bodham for his kindness to my Homer; and with my love to you all, and with Mrs. Unwin's kind respects, am,

My dear, dear Rose, ever yours.

P. S. — I mourn the death of your poor brother Castres, whom I should have seen had he lived, and should have seen with the greatest pleasure. He was an amiable boy, and I was very fond of him.

Still another P. S. — I find, on consulting Mrs. Unwin, that I have underrated our capabilities, and that we have not only room for you and Mr. Bodham, but for two of your sex, and even for your nephew into the bargain. We shall be happy to have it all so occupied. Your nephew tells me that his sister, in the qualities of her mind, resembles you; that is enough to make her dear to me, and I beg you will assure her that she is so. Let it not be long before I hear from you.

XCIII.

CONCERNING THE TWO POEMS WHICH GAVE HIM THE MOST PLEASURE IN THE WRITING.

To Mrs. King.

WESTON UNDERWOOD, *March* 12, 1790.

MY DEAR MADAM, — I live in such a nook, have so few opportunities of hearing news, and so little time to read it, that to me to begin a letter seems always a sort of forlorn hope. Can it be possible, I say to myself, that I should have anything to communicate? These misgivings have an ill effect, so far as my punctuality is concerned, and are apt to deter me from the business of letter-writing as from an enterprise altogether impracticable.

I will not say that you are more pleased with my trifles than they deserve, lest I should seem to call your judgment in question; but I suspect that a little partiality to the brother of my brother enters into the opinion you form of them. No matter, however, by what you are influenced, it is for my interest that you should like them at any rate, because, such as they are, they are the only return that I can make you for all your kindness. This consideration will have two effects: it will have a tendency to make me more industrious in the production of such pieces, and more attentive to the manner in which I write them. This reminds me of a piece in your possession, which I entreat you to commit to the flames, because I am somewhat ashamed of it. To make you amends I hereby promise to send you a new edition of it when time shall serve, delivered from the passages that I dislike in the first, and in other respects amended. The piece that I mean is one entitled "To Lady Hesketh on her furnishing for me our house at Weston," or, as the lawyers say, words to that amount. I have likewise, since I sent you the last packet, been delivered of two or three other brats, and, as the year proceeds, shall probably add to the number. All that come shall be basketed in time, and conveyed to your door.

I have lately received from a female cousin of mine in Norfolk, whom I have not seen these thirty years, a picture of my own mother. She died when I wanted two days of being six years old; yet I remember her perfectly, find the picture a strong likeness of her, because her memory has been ever precious to me, have written a poem on the receipt of it,[1] — a poem which, one excepted,[2] I had more pleasure in writing than any that I ever wrote. That

[1] On the Receipt of my Mother's Picture out of Norfolk.
[2] Probably the sonnet beginning, "Mary! I want a lyre with other strings."

one was addressed to a lady whom I expect in a few minutes to come down to breakfast, and who has supplied to me the place of my own mother — my own invaluable mother — these six-and-twenty years. Some sons may be said to have had many fathers; but a plurality of mothers is not common.

Adieu, my dear madam. Be assured that I always think of you with much esteem and affection, and am, with mine and Mrs. Unwin's best compliments to you and yours, most unfeignedly your friend and humble servant.

XCIV.

CHANGE OF STYLE IN HIS HOMER TRANSLATION.

To Lady Hesketh.

THE LODGE, *March* 22, 1790.

I REJOICE, my dearest cousin, that my MSS. have roamed the earth so successfully, and have met with no disaster. The single book excepted that went to the bottom of the Thames and rose again, they have been fortunate without exception. I am not superstitious, but have nevertheless as good a right to believe that adventure an omen, and a favorable one, as Swift had to interpret, as he did, the loss of a fine fish, which he had no sooner laid on the bank than it flounced into the water again. This, he tells us himself, he always considered as a type of his future disappointments. And why may not I as well consider the marvellous recovery of my lost book from the bottom of the Thames as typical of its future prosperity? To say the truth, I have no fears now about the success of my Translation, though in time past I have had many. I knew there was a style somewhere, could I but find it, in which Homer ought to be rendered, and which alone would suit him. Long time I blundered about it ere I could attain to any decided judgment on the matter. At first I was betrayed by a desire of accommodating my language to the simplicity of his into much of the quaintness that belonged to our writers of the fifteenth century. In the course of many revisals I have delivered myself from this evil, I believe, entirely; but I have done it slowly, and as a man separates himself from his mistress when he is going to marry. I had so strong a predilection in favor of this style at first that I was crazed to find that others were not as much enamoured with it as myself. At every passage of that sort which I obliterated, I groaned bitterly, and said to myself, "I am spoiling my work to please those who have no taste for the simple graces of antiquity." But in measure, as I adopted a more modern phraseology, I became a convert to their opinion; and in the last revisal, which I am now making, am not sensible of having spared a single expression of the obsolete kind. I see my work so much improved by this alteration that I am filled with wonder at my own backwardness to assent to the necessity of it, and the more when I consider that Milton, with whose manner I account myself intimately acquainted, is never quaint, never twangs through the nose, but is everywhere grand

and elegant, without resorting to musty antiquity for his beauties. On the contrary, he took a long stride forward, left the language of his own day far behind him, and anticipated the expressions of a century yet to come.

I have now, as I said, no longer any doubt of the event; but I will give thee a shilling if thou wilt tell me what I shall say in my Preface. It is an affair of much delicacy, and I have as many opinions about it as there are whims in a weathercock.

Send my MSS. and thine when thou wilt. In a day or two I shall enter on the last Iliad. When I have finished it I shall give the Odyssey one more reading, and shall therefore shortly have occasion for the copy in thy possession; but you see that there is no need to hurry.

XCV.

FORBIDDING ANY APPLICATION FOR THE LAUREATE-SHIP.

To Lady Hesketh.

THE LODGE, *May* 28, 1790.

MY DEAREST COZ, — I thank thee for the offer of thy best services on this occasion.[1] But Heaven guard my brows from the wreath you mention, whatever wreath beside may hereafter adorn them! It would be a leaden extinguisher clapped on all the fire of my genius, and I should never more produce

[1] Warton had died, leaving vacant the post of poet-laureate, and Lady Hesketh had wished to procure it for Cowper.

a line worth reading. To speak seriously, it would make me miserable, and therefore I am sure that thou, of all my friends, would least wish me to wear it.

Adieu! Ever thine — in Homer-hurry.

XCVI.

COMMENTS ON THE FRENCH REVOLUTION.

To Lady Hesketh.

July 7, 1790.

INSTEAD of beginning with the saffron-vested morning to which Homer invites me, on a morning that has no saffron vest to boast, I shall begin with you.

It is irksome to us both to wait so long as we must for you; but we are willing to hope that by a longer stay you will make us amends for all this tedious procrastination.

Mrs. Unwin has made known her whole case to Mr. Gregson, whose opinion of it has been very consolatory to me. He says, indeed, it is a case perfectly out of the reach of all physical aid, but at the same time not at all dangerous. Constant pain is a sad grievance, whatever part is affected, and she is hardly ever free from an aching head, as well as an uneasy side; but patience is an anodyne of God's own preparation, and of that he gives her largely.

The French, who, like all lively folks, are extreme in everything, are such in their zeal for freedom;

and if it were possible to make so noble a cause ridiculous, their manner of promoting it could not fail to do so. Princes and peers reduced to plain gentlemanship, and gentles reduced to a level with their own lackeys, are excesses of which they will repent hereafter. Differences of rank and subordination are, I believe, of God's appointment, and consequently essential to the well-being of society; but what we mean by fanaticism in religion is exactly that which animates their politics; and unless time should sober them, they will, after all, be an unhappy people. Perhaps it deserves not much to be wondered at that at their first escape from tyrannic shackles they should act extravagantly, and treat their kings as they have sometimes treated their idols. To these, however, they are reconciled in due time again; but their respect for monarchy is at an end. They want nothing now but a little English sobriety, and that they want extremely. I heartily wish them some wit in their anger, for it were great pity that so many millions should be miserable for want of it.

XCVII.

ON SENDING HIS HOMER TRANSLATION TO THE PUBLISHER.

To Mrs. Bodham.

Weston, *September* 9, 1790.

My dearest Cousin, — I am truly sorry to be forced, after all, to resign the hope of seeing you and Mr. Bodham at Weston this year; the next may possibly be more propitious, and I heartily wish it may. Poor Catharine's unseasonable indisposition has also cost us a disappointment, which we much regret; and were it not that Johnny[2] has made shift to reach us, we should think ourselves completely unfortunate. But him we have, and him we will hold as long as we can; so expect not very soon to see him in Norfolk. He is so harmless, cheerful, gentle, and good-tempered, and I am so entirely at my ease with him, that I cannot surrender him without a *needs must,* even to those who have a superior claim upon him. He left us yesterday morning, and whither do you think he is gone, and on what errand? Gone, as sure as you are alive, to London, and to convey my Homer to the bookseller's. But he will return the day after to-morrow, and I mean to part with him no more till necessity shall force us asunder. Suspect me not, my cousin, of being such a monster as to have imposed this task myself on your kind nephew, or even to have thought of doing it. It happened that one day, as we chatted by the fireside, I expressed a wish that I could hear of some trusty body going to London to whose care I might consign my voluminous labors, — the work of five years. For I purpose never to visit that city again myself, and should have been uneasy to have left a charge of so much importance to me altogether to the care of a stage-coachman. Johnny had no

[1] Catharine Johnson, sister of John Johnson.
[2] John Johnson, who had now become one of Cowper's most devoted friends and helpers.

sooner heard my wish than, offering himself to the service, he fulfilled it; and his offer was made in such terms, and accompanied with a countenance and manner expressive of so much alacrity, that unreasonable as I thought it at first to give him so much trouble, I soon found that I should mortify him by a refusal. He is gone, therefore, with a box full of poetry, of which I think nobody will plunder him. He has only to say what it is, and there is no commodity I think a freebooter would covet less.

XCVIII.

EPIGRAM ON THE ILL SUCCESS OF HIS SUBSCRIPTION AT OXFORD.

To Mrs. Throckmorton.

April 1, 1791.

MY DEAR MRS. FROG,[1] — A word or two before breakfast, which is all that I shall have time to send you. You have not, I hope, forgot to tell Mr. Frog how much I am obliged to him for his kind, though unsuccessful, attempt in my favor at Oxford. It seems not a little extraordinary that persons so nobly patronized themselves on the score of literature should resolve to give no encouragement to it in return. Should I find a fair opportunity to thank them hereafter, I will not neglect it.

[1] Cowper's pet title for the Throckmortons was Mr. and Mrs. Frog.

> Could Homer come himself, distress'd and poor,
> And tune his harp at Rhedycina's door,
> The rich old vixen would exclaim (I fear),
> "Begone! no tramper gets a farthing here."

I have read your husband's pamphlet through and through. You may think, perhaps, and so may he, that a question so remote from all concern of mine could not interest me; but if you think so, you are both mistaken. He can write nothing that will not interest me, in the first place for the writer's sake, and in the next place because he writes better and reasons better than anybody, — with more candor and with more sufficiency, and consequently with more satisfaction to all his readers, save only his opponents. They, I think, by this time wish that they had let him alone.

Tom is delighted past measure with his wooden nag, and gallops at a rate that would kill any horse that had a life to lose.

Adieu!

XCIX.

SUCCESS OF HIS HOMER. — CORRESPONDENCE WITH THURLOW CONCERNING IT.

To Lady Hesketh.

THE LODGE, *August* 30, 1791.

MY DEAREST COZ, — The walls of Ogressa's chamber shall be furnished as elegantly as they can be, and at little cost; and when you see them you shall cry "Bravo!" Bedding we have, but two chairs will be wanting, the servants' hall having engaged all our supernumeraries. These you will either send, or give us commission to buy them. Such as will suit may be found probably at Maurice Smith's, of house-furnishing memory; and this latter course I should think the best, because they are of all things most liable to fracture in a wagon.

I know not how it can have happened that Homer is such a secret at Tunbridge, for I can tell you that his fame is on the wing, and flies rapidly. Johnson, however, seems to be clear from blame; and when you recollect that the whole edition is his by purchase, and that he has no possible way to get his money again but by the sale of it, thou thyself wilt think so. A tradesman — an old stager too — may surely be trusted with his own interest.

I have spoken big words about Homer's fame, and bigger, perhaps, than my intelligence will justify, for I have not heard much; but what I have heard has been pretty much to the purpose. First, little Johnny, going through Cambridge, in his way home, learned from his tutor there that it had found many admirers amongst the best qualified judges of that university, and that they were very liberal of their praises. Secondly, Mr. Rye wrote me word lately that a certain candid fair critic and excellent judge, of the county of Northampton, gives it high encomiums. Thirdly, Mr. Rye came over himself from Gayhurst yesterday on purpose to tell me how much he was delighted with it. He had just been reading the sixth Iliad, and comparing it with Pope and with the original, and professed himself enchanted. Fourthly, Mr. Frog is much pleased with it; and fifthly, Henry Cowper is bewitched with it; and sixthly, so are — you and I, — *ça suffit.*

But now if thou hast the faculty of erecting thy ears, lift them into the air, first taking off thy cap, that they may have the highest possible elevation. Mrs. Unwin says, No, don't tell her ladyship all, tell her only enough to raise her curiosity, that she may come the sooner to Weston to have it gratified. But I say, Yes, I will tell her all, lest she should be overcharged, and burst by the way.

The Chancellor and I, my dear, have had a correspondence on the subject of Homer. He had doubts, it seems, about the propriety of translating him in blank verse, and wrote to Henry to tell him so, adding a translation of his own in rhyme of the speech of Achilles to Phœnix, in the ninth book; and referring him to me, who, he said, could elevate it and polish it and give it the tone of Homer. Henry sent this letter to me, and I answered it in one to his Lordship, but not meddling with his verses, for I remembered what happened between Gil Blas and the Archbishop of Toledo. His Lordship sent me two sheets in reply, filled with arguments in favor of rhyme, which I was to answer if I could, and containing another translation of the same passage, only in blank verse, leaving it to me to give it rhyme, to make it close and faithful and poetical. All this I performed as best I could; and yesterday I heard from him again. In this last letter he says, "I am clearly convinced that

Homer may be best translated *without* rhyme, and that you have succeeded in the passages I have looked into."

Such is the candor of a wise man and a real scholar. I would to Heaven that all prejudiced persons were like him! — I answered this letter immediately; and here, I suppose, our correspondence ends. Have I not made a great convert? You shall see the letters, both his and mine, when you come.

My picture hangs in the study. I will not tell thee what others think of it, but thou shalt judge for thyself. I altogether approve Mrs. Carter's sentiments upon the Birmingham riots, and admire her manner of expressing them. The Frogs came down to-day, bringing Cátharina with them. Mrs. Frog has caught cold, as I hear, in her journey; therefore how she may be now, I know not, but before she went she was well and in excellent spirits. I rejoice that thy poor lungs can play freely, and shall be happy when they can do the same at Weston. My eyes are weak, and somewhat inflamed, and have never been well this month past.

Mrs. Unwin is tolerably well, — that is, much as usual. She joins me in best love, and in everything that you can wish us both to feel for you.

Adieu, my dearest coz,

Ever thine.

C.

ENGAGEMENT TO EDIT MILTON.

To Samuel Rose, Esq.

THE LODGE, *September* 14, 1791.

MY DEAR FRIEND, — Whoever reviews me will in fact have a laborious task of it, in the performance of which he ought to move leisurely, and to exercise much critical discernment. In the mean time my courage is kept up by the arrival of such testimonies in my favor as give me the greatest pleasure, coming from quarters the most respectable. I have reason, therefore, to hope that our periodical judges will not be very adverse to me, and that perhaps they may even favor me. If one man of taste and letters is pleased, another man so qualified can hardly be displeased; and if critics of a different description grumble, they will not, however, materially hurt me.

You, who know how necessary it is to me to be employed, will be glad to hear that I have been called to a new literary engagement, and that I have not refused it. A Milton that is to rival, and if possible to exceed, in splendor Boydell's Shakespeare, is in contemplation, and I am in the editor's office. Fuseli is the painter. My business will be to select notes from others and to write original notes, to translate the Latin and Italian poems, and to give a correct text. I shall have years allowed me to do it in.

CI.

MRS. UNWIN STRICKEN WITH PARALYSIS.

To Samuel Rose, Esq.

The Lodge, *December* 21, 1791.

My dear Friend, — It grieves me, after having indulged a little hope that I might see you in the holidays, to be obliged to disappoint myself. The occasion, too, is such as will insure me your sympathy.

On Saturday last, while I was at my desk near the window, and Mrs. Unwin at the fireside opposite to it, I heard her suddenly exclaim, "Oh, Mr. Cowper, don't let me fall!" I turned and saw her actually falling, together with her chair, and started to her side just in time to prevent her. She was seized with a violent giddiness, which lasted, though with some abatement, the whole day, and was attended, too, with some other very, very alarming symptoms. At present, however, she is relieved from the vertigo, and seems in all respects better.

She has been my faithful and affectionate nurse for many years, and consequently has a claim on all my attentions. She has them, and will have them as long as she wants them, — which will probably be, at the best, a considerable time to come. I feel the shock, as you may suppose, in every nerve. God grant that there may be no repetition of it! Another such a stroke upon her would, I think, overset me completely; but at present I hold up bravely.

CII.

LINES FOR MISS PATTY MORE'S ALBUM.—DEPARTURE OF THE THROCKMORTONS FROM WESTON.

To the Rev. John Newton.

WESTON, *March* 4, 1792.

MY DEAR FRIEND,— My patience must indeed have been made of flimsy stuff had it given way to your reasonable objection. Yours is likely to undergo a severer trial while I pester you again on this trivial subject.

You and I were well content with the new edition of my four lines as corrected and amended by my cousin. You even thought that they could not be mended; but she was of a different opinion, and has given a copy of them I think still better. Unless, therefore, you have already sent them, I shall be obliged to you if you will not till I can remit to you this best edition, which I shall soon be able to do by the aid of my cousin, who goes to town on Wednesday. They are at present thus altered:—

> In vain to live from age to age,
> While modern bards endeavor,
> *I* write my name in Patty's page,
> And gain my point forever.

The greater propriety of this way of expressing it will present itself to you, and therefore need not be mentioned.

You may dismiss all fears lest I should bestow praise on so unworthy a subject of it as his R. H.

Whatever I may write on that occasion shall, you may depend on it, do him as little honor and as much justice as the lines you sent me. I have paid here and there a compliment to persons who I knew deserved one, and I would not invalidate them all by proving that my Muse is an indiscriminating harlot, and her good word nothing worth.

All our little world is going to London, — the gulf that swallows most of our good things, and, like a bad stomach, too often assimilates them to itself. Our neighbors at the Hall go thither to-morrow. Mr. and Mrs. Throckmorton, as we lately called them, but now Sir John and my Lady, are no longer inhabitants here, but henceforth of Bucklands, in Berkshire. I feel the loss of them, and shall feel it, since kinder or more friendly treatment I never can receive at any hands than I have always found at theirs. But it has long been a foreseen change, and was indeed almost daily expected long before it happened. The desertion of the Hall, however, will not be total. The second brother, George, now Mr. Courtenay, intends to reside there; and with him, as with his elder brother, I have always been on terms the most agreeable.

Such is this variable scene, — so variable that, had the reflections I sometimes make upon it a permanent influence, I should tremble at the thought of a new connection, and, to be out of the reach of its mutability, lead almost the life of a hermit. It is well with those who, like you, have God for their companion. Death cannot deprive them of him, and he changes not his place of abode. Other changes, therefore, to them are all supportable; and what you say of your own experience is the strongest possible proof of it. Had you lived without God, you could not have endured the loss you mention. May he preserve me from a similar one, — at least till he shall be pleased to draw me to himself again. Then, if ever that day come, it will make me equal to any burden; but at present I can bear nothing well. Adieu! Mrs. Unwin is, I hope, daily regaining strength, and joins me in love to yourself and Betsy. Lady Hesketh sends compliments. I am sincerely yours.

CIII.

BEGINNING OF FRIENDSHIP WITH WILLIAM HAYLEY.

To Lady Hesketh.

THE LODGE, *March* 25, 1792.

MY DEAREST COZ, — Mr. Rose's longer stay than he at first intended was the occasion of the longer delay of my answer to your note, as you may both have perceived by the date thereof, and learned from his information. It was a daily trouble to me to see it lying in the window-seat, while I knew you were in expectation of its arrival. By this time I presume you have seen him, and have seen likewise Mr. Hayley's friendly letter and complimentary sonnet,[1] as well as the letter of the honest Quaker, —

[1] Hayley was engaged in writing a Life of Milton for a Boydell edition of Milton's works. A newspaper report that the rivalry of the publishers was shared also by the writers,

all of which, at least the two former, I shall be glad to receive again at a fair opportunity. Mr. Hayley's letter slept six weeks in Johnson's custody. It was necessary I should answer it without delay, and accordingly I answered it the very evening on which I received it, giving him to understand, among other things, how much vexation the bookseller's folly had cost me, who had detained it so long, — especially on account of the distress that I knew it must have occasioned to him also. From his reply, which the return of the post brought me, I learn that in the long interval of my non-correspondence he had suffered anxiety and mortification enough, — so much that I dare say he made twenty vows never to hazard again either letter or compliment to an unknown author. What indeed could he imagine less, than that I meant by such an obstinate silence to tell him that I valued neither him nor his praises nor his proffered friendship, — in short, that I considered him as a rival, and therefore, like a true author, hated and despised him? He is now, however, convinced that I love him, — as indeed I do, and I account him the chief acquisition that my own verse has ever procured me. Brute should I be if I did not; for he promises me every assistance in his power.

I have likewise a very pleasing letter from Mr. Park, which I wish you were here to read, and a very pleasing poem that came inclosed in it

led Hayley to address a generous letter and complimentary sonnet to Cowper, through the medium of his publisher, Johnson.

for my revisal, written when he was only twenty years of age, yet wonderfully well written, though wanting some correction.

To Mr. Hurdis I return "Sir Thomas More"[1] to-morrow; having revised it a second time. He is now a very respectable figure, and will do my friend, who gives him to the public this spring, considerable credit.

CIV.

SUDDEN FRIENDSHIPS. — INVITATION TO WESTON.

To William Hayley, Esq.

WESTON, *April* 6, 1792.

MY DEAR FRIEND, — God grant that this friendship of ours may be a comfort to us all the rest of our days, in a world where true friendships are rarities, and especially where, suddenly formed, they are apt soon to terminate! But, as I said before, I feel a disposition of heart toward you that I never felt for one whom I had never seen; and that shall prove itself, I trust, in the event a propitious omen.

. . . . . .

Horace says somewhere, though I may quote it amiss, perhaps, for I have a terrible memory, —

*Utrumque nostrum incredibili modo
Consentit astrum* ———.

[1] A tragedy written by Mr. Hurdis, and submitted to Cowper for criticism.

... Our *stars consent*, at least have had an influence somewhat similar in another and more important article. ——...

It gives me the sincerest pleasure that I may hope to see you at Weston; for as to any migrations of mine, they must, I fear, notwithstanding the joy I should feel in being a guest of yours, be still considered in the light of impossibilities. Come then, my friend, and be as welcome, as the country people say here, as the flowers in May. I am happy, as I say, in the expectation; but the fear, or rather the consciousness, that I shall not answer on a nearer view, makes it a trembling kind of happiness, and a doubtful.

After the privacy which I have mentioned above, I went to Huntingdon. Soon after my arrival there I took up my quarters at the house of the Rev. Mr. Unwin; I lived with him while he lived, and ever since his death have lived with his widow. Her, therefore, you will find mistress of the house; and I judge of you amiss or you will find her just such as you would wish. To me she has been often a nurse, and invariably the kindest friend through a thousand adversities that I have had to grapple with in the course of almost thirty years. I thought it better to introduce her to you thus than to present her to you at your coming, quite a stranger.

Bring with you any books that you think may be useful to my commentatorship; for with you for an 'interpreter I shall be afraid of none of them; and in truth, if you think that you shall want them, you must bring books for your own use also, for they are an article with which I am *heinously unprovided*, being much in the condition of the man whose library Pope describes as —

"No mighty store,
His own works neatly bound, and little more!"

You shall know how this has come to pass hereafter.

Tell me, my friend, are your letters in your own handwriting? If so, I am in pain for your eyes, lest by such frequent demands upon them I should hurt them. I had rather write you three letters for one, much as I prize your letters, than *that* should happen. And now, for the present, adieu. I am going to accompany Milton into the lake of fire and brimstone, having just begun my annotations.

CV.

MRS. UNWIN'S SECOND PARALYTIC STROKE.

To Lady Hesketh.

WESTON, *May* 24, 1792.

I WISH with all my heart, my dearest Coz, that I had not ill news for the subject of the present letter. My friend, my Mary, has again been attacked by the same disorder that threatened me last year with the loss of her, and of which you were yourself a witness. Gregson would not allow that first stroke to be paralytic, but this he acknowledges to be so; and with respect to the former, I never had myself any doubt that it was; but this has been much the severest. Her speech has been almost unintelligible from the moment that she was struck; it is with difficulty that she opens her eyes, and she cannot keep them open, the muscles necessary to the purpose being contracted; and as to self-moving powers from place to place and the use of her right hand and arm, — she has entirely lost them.

It has happened well that, of all men living, the man most qualified to assist and comfort me is here, though till within these few days I never saw him, and a few weeks since had no expectation that I ever should. You have already guessed that I mean Hayley, — Hayley, who loves me as if he had known me from my cradle. When he returns to town, as he must, alas! too soon, he will pay his respects to you.

I will not conclude without adding that our poor patient is beginning, I hope, to recover from this stroke also; but her amendment is slow, as must be expected at her time of life, and in such a disorder. I am as well myself as you have ever known me in a time of much trouble, and even better.

CVI.

EVENTFULNESS OF THE LAST TWO MONTHS.

To Lady Hesketh.

WESTON, *June* 11, 1792.

MY DEAREST COZ, — Thou art ever in my thoughts, whether I am writing to thee or not; and my correspondence seems to grow upon me at such a rate that I am not able to address thee so often as I would; in fact, I live only to write letters. Hayley is, as you see, added to the number; and to him I write almost as daily as I rise in the morning; nor is he only added, but his friend Carwardine also, — Carwardine the generous, the disinterested, the friendly. I seem, in short, to have stumbled suddenly on a race of heroes, — men who resolve to have no interests of their own till mine are served.

But I will proceed to other matters that concern me more intimately and more immediately than all that can be done for me either by the great or the small, or by both united. Since I wrote last, Mrs. Unwin has been continually improving in strength, but at so gradual a rate that I can only mark it by saying that she moves about every day with less support than the former. Her recovery is most of all retarded by want of sleep. On the whole, I believe she goes on as well as could be expected, though not quite well enough to satisfy me; and Dr. Austin, speaking from the reports I have made of her, says he has no doubt of her restoration.

During the last two months I seem to myself to have been in a dream. It has been a most eventful period, and fruitful to an uncommon degree both in good and evil. I have been very ill and suffered excruciating pain. I recovered, and became quite well again. I received within my doors a man but lately an entire stranger, and who now loves me as his brother, and forgets himself to serve me. Mrs. Unwin has been seized with an illness that for many days threatened to deprive me of her, and to cast a gloom — an impenetrable one — on all my future prospects. She is now granted to me again. A few days since I should have thought the moon might have descended into my purse as lightly as any emolument, and now it seems not impossible. All this has come to pass with such rapidity as events move with in romance, indeed, but not often in real life. Events of all sorts creep or fly exactly as God pleases.

To the foregoing I have to add, in conclusion, the arrival of my Johnny[1] just when I wanted him most, and when only a few days before I had no expectation of him. He came to dinner on Saturday, and I hope I shall keep him long. What comes next I know not, but shall endeavor, as you exhort me, to look for good, and I know I shall have your prayers that I may not be disappointed.

Hayley tells me you begin to be jealous of him, lest I should love him more than I love you, and bids me say "that should I do so, you in revenge must love him more than I do." — Him I know you will love, and me because you have such a habit of doing it that you cannot help it.

Adieu! My knuckles ache with letter-writing. With my poor patient's affectionate remembrances, and Johnny's,

I am ever thine.

[1] Cowper's nephew, Rev. John Johnson; on him was soon to devolve the entire responsibility of caring for Cowper and Mrs. Unwin through their declining years and failing powers.

CVII.

HIS PUBLISHER'S GOOD INTENTIONS. — POLITICS.

To Lady Hesketh.

December 1, 1792.

I AM truly glad, my dearest coz, that the waters of Cheltenham have done thee good, and wish ardently that those of Bath may establish thy health, and prove the means of prolonging it many years, even till thou shalt become what thou wast called at a very early age, an old wench indeed. I have been a *pauvre misérable* ever since I came from Eartham, and was little better while there; so that whatever motive may incline me to travel again hereafter, it will not be the hope that my spirits will be much the better for it. Neither was Mrs. Unwin's health so much improved by that frisk of ours into Sussex, as I had hoped and expected. She is, however, tolerably well, but very far indeed from having recovered the effects of her last disorder.

My birthday — the sixty-first that I have numbered — has proved for once a propitious day to me; for on that day my spirits began to mend, — my nights became less hideous, and my days have been such of course.

I have heard nothing from Joseph, and having been always used to hear from him in November, am reduced to the dire necessity of supposing, with you, that he is heinously offended. Being in want of money, however, I wrote to him yesterday, and a letter which ought to produce a friendly answer; but whether it will or not is an affair at present of great uncertainty. Walter Bagot is offended too, and wonders that I would have any connection with so bad a man as the author of the Essay on Old Maids must necessarily be. Poor man! he has five sisters, I think, in that predicament, which makes *his* resentment rather excusable. Joseph, by the way, has two, and perhaps may be proportionally influenced by that consideration. Should that be the case, I have nothing left to do but to wish them all good husbands, since the reconciliation of my two friends seems closely connected with that contingency.

In making the first advances to your sister you have acted like yourself, — that is to say, like a good and affectionate sister, and will not, I hope, lose your reward. Rewarded in another world you will be, no doubt; but I should hope that you will be not altogether unrecompensed in this. Thou hast a heart, I know, that cannot endure to be long at enmity with any one; and were I capable of using thee never so ill, I am sure that in time you would sue to me for a pardon. Thou dost not want fire, but meekness is predominant in thee.

I was never so idle in my life, and never had so much to do. God knows when this will end, but I think of bestirring myself soon, and of putting on my Miltonic trammels once again. That once done, I shall not, I hope, put them off till the work is finished. I have written nothing lately but a sonnet to Romney,[1] and a mortuary copy of verses for the

[1] The artist who had just painted Cowper's portrait.

town of Northampton, having been applied to by the new clerk for that purpose.

Johnson designs handsomely. You must pardon Johnson, and receive him into your best graces. He purposes to publish, together with my Homer, a new edition of my two volumes of poems, and to make me a present of the entire profits. They are to be handsome quartos, with an engraving of Abbott's picture of me prefixed. I have left myself neither time nor room for politics.

The French are a vain and childish people, and conduct themselves on this grand occasion with a levity and extravagance nearly akin to madness; but it would have been better for Austria and Prussia to let them alone. All nations have a right to choose their own mode of government; and the sovereignty of the people is a doctrine that evinces itself; for whenever the people choose to be masters, they always are so, and none can hinder them. God grant that we may have no revolution here; but unless we have a reform, we certainly shall. Depend upon it, my dear, the hour is come when power founded in patronage and corrupt majorities must govern this land no longer. Concessions, too, must be made to dissenters of every denomination. They have a right to them, — a right to all the privileges of Englishmen; and sooner or later, by fair means or by force, they will have them.

Adieu, my dearest coz. I have only time to add Mrs. U.'s most affectionate remembrances, and to conclude myself

Ever thine.

Mr. and Mrs. Rose came on the twenty-second, and Johnny with them, — the former to stay ten days. It is strange that anybody should suspect Mr. Smith of having been assisted by me. None writes more rapidly or more correctly, — twenty pages in a morning, which I have often read and heard read at night, and found not a word to alter. This moment comes a very kind letter from Joseph. Sephus tells me I may expect to see very soon the strongest assurances from the people of property of every description to support the King and present constitution. In this I do most sincerely rejoice, as you will. He wishes to know my political opinions, and he shall most truly.

CVIII.

ANNOTATIONS OF HOMER.

To Samuel Rose, Esq.

May 5, 1793.

MY DEAR FRIEND, — My delay to answer your last kind letter, to which likewise you desired a speedy reply, must have seemed rather difficult to explain on any other supposition than that of illness; but illness has not been the cause, — although, to say the truth, I cannot boast of having been lately very well. Yet has not this been the cause of my silence, but your own advice — very proper, and earnestly given to me — to proceed in the revisal of Homer. To this it is owing that, instead of giving an hour or two before breakfast to my correspondence, I allot that time entirely to my studies. I have nearly given the last touches to the poetry, and am now busied far more laboriously in writing notes at the request of my honest bookseller, transmitted to me in the first instance by you, and afterwards repeated by himself. I am therefore deep in the old Scholia, and have advanced to the latter part of Iliad nine, explaining as I go such passages as may be difficult to unlearned readers, and such only; for notes of that kind are the notes that Johnson desired. I find it a more laborious task than the translation was, and shall be heartily glad when it is over. In the mean time all the letters I have received remain unanswered, or if they receive an answer, it is always a short one. Such this must be. Johnny is here, having flown over London.

Homer, I believe, will make a much more respectable appearance than before. Johnson now thinks it will be right to make a separate impression of the amendments.

I breakfast every morning on seven or eight pages of the Greek commentators; for so much I am obliged to read in order to select perhaps three or four short notes for the readers of my translation.

Homer is indeed a tie upon me that must not on any account be broken till all his demands are satisfied; though I have fancied while the revisal of the Odyssey was at a distance that it would ask less labor in the finishing, it is not unlikely that, when I take it actually in hand, I may find myself mistaken. Of this, at least, I am sure, that uneven verse abounds much more in it than it once did in the Iliad; yet to the latter the critics objected on that account, though to the former never, — perhaps because they had not read it. Hereafter they shall not quarrel with me on that score. The Iliad is now all smooth turnpike, and I will take equal care that there shall be no jolts in the Odyssey.

CIX.

INTRUSIVE STRANGERS. — LITERARY CO-OPERATION.

To William Hayley, Esq.

WESTON, *October* 5, 1793.

MY good intentions towards you, my dearest brother, are continually frustrated, and (which is most provoking) not by such engagements and avocations as have a right to my attention, such as those to my Mary and to the old bard of Greece, but by mere impertinencies, — such as calls of civility from persons not very interesting to me, and letters from a distance still less interesting, because the writers of them are strangers. A man sent me a long copy of verses, which I could do no less than acknowledge. They were silly enough, and cost me eighteen pence, — which was seventeen pence halfpenny farthing more than they were worth. Another sent me at the same time a plan, requesting my opinion of it, and that I would lend him my name as editor, — a request with which I shall not comply; but I am obliged to tell him so; and one letter is all that I have time to despatch in a day, sometimes half a one, and sometimes I am not able to write at all. Thus it is that my time perishes, and I can neither give so much of it as I would to you or to any other valuable purpose.

On Tuesday we expect company, — Mr. Rose and Lawrence the painter. Yet once more is my patience to be exercised, and once more I am made to wish that my face had been movable, to put on and take off at pleasure, so as to be portable in a bandbox, and sent to the artist. These, however, will be gone, as I believe I told you, before you arrive, at which time I know not that anybody will be here, — except my Johnny, whose presence will not at all interfere with our readings. You will not, I believe, find me a very slashing critic; I hardly indeed expect to find anything in your Life of Milton that I shall sentence to amputation. How should it be too long? A well-written work, sensible and spirited, such as yours was when I saw it, is never so. But, however, we shall see. I promise to spare nothing that I think may be lopped off with advantage.

I began this letter yesterday, but could not finish it till now. I have risen this morning like an infernal frog out of Acheron, covered with the ooze and mud of melancholy. For this reason I am not sorry to find myself at the bottom of my paper; for had I more room perhaps I might fill it all with croaking, and make an heart ache at Eartham[1] which I wish to be always cheerful. Adieu. My poor sympathizing Mary is of course sad, but always mindful of you.

Eartham was Hayley's home at this time.

CX.

PRINCIPLES OF TRANSLATION.

To William Hayley, Esq.

WESTON, *January* 5, 1794.

MY DEAR HAYLEY, — I have waited, but waited in vain, for a propitious moment when I might give my old friend's objections[1] the consideration they deserve; I shall at last be forced to send a vague answer, unworthy to be sent to a person accustomed, like him, to close reasoning and abstruse discussion, for I rise after ill rest, and with a frame of mind perfectly unsuited to the occasion. I sit too at the window for light's sake, where I am so cold that my pen slips out of my fingers. First I will give you a translation *de novo* of this untranslatable prayer. It is shaped as nearly as I could contrive to his Lordship's ideas; but I have little hope that it will satisfy him : —

> Grant, Jove, and all ye gods, that this my son
> Be, as myself have been, illustrious here!
> A valiant man! and let him reign in Troy;
> May all who witness his return from fight
> Hereafter, say, — he far excels his sire;
> And let him bring back gory trophies, stripp'd
> From foes slain by him, to his mother's joy.

---

[1] Chancellor Thurlow had criticized Cowper's version of certain Homer lines, and both he and Hayley had submitted to their friend translations of their own as improvements.

Imlac, in "Rasselas," says (I forget to whom), "You have convinced me that it is impossible to be a poet." In like manner I might say to his Lordship, "You have convinced me that it is impossible to be a translator." To be a translator, on his terms, at least, is, I am sure, impossible; on his terms I would defy Homer himself, were he alive, to translate the Paradise Lost into Greek. Yet Milton had Homer much in his eye when he composed that poem; whereas Homer never thought of me or my translation. There are minutiæ in every language which transfused into another will spoil the version. Such extreme fidelity is in fact unfaithful; such close resemblance takes away all likeness. The original is elegant, easy, natural; the copy is clumsy, constrained, unnatural. To what is this owing? To the adoption of terms not congenial to your purpose, and of a context such as no man writing an original work would make use of. Homer is everything that a poet should be. A translation of Homer so made will be everything that a translation of Homer should not be; because it will be written in no language under heaven, — it will be English and it will be Greek, and therefore it will be neither. He is the man, whoever he be (I do not pretend to be that man myself), — he is the man best qualified as a translator of Homer who has drenched and steeped and soaked himself in the effusions of his genius till he has imbibed their color to the bone, and who when he is thus dyed through and through, distinguishing between what is essentially Greek and what may be habited in English, rejects the former and is faithful to the latter as far as the purposes of fine poetry will permit, and no further: this, I think, may be easily proved. Homer is everywhere remarkable either for ease, dignity, or energy of expression, for grandeur of conception, and a majestic flow of numbers. If we copy him so closely as to make every one of these excellent properties of his absolutely unattainable, — which will certainly be the effect of too close a copy, — instead of translating, we murder him. Therefore, after all that his Lordship has said, I still hold freedom to be an indispensable, — freedom, I mean, with respect to the expression; freedom so limited as never to leave behind the *matter*, but at the same time indulged with a sufficient scope to secure the spirit, and as much as possible of the manner. I say as much as possible, because an English manner must differ from a Greek one in order to be graceful; and for this there is no remedy. Can an ungraceful, awkward translation of Homer be a good one? No. But a graceful, easy, natural, faithful version of him, will not that be a good one? Yes. Allow me but this, and I insist upon it that such a one may be produced on my principles, and can be produced on no other.

I have not had time to criticise his Lordship's other version. You know how little time I have for anything, and can tell him so.

Adieu, my dear brother. I have now tired both you and myself, and, with the love of the whole trio, remain,

Yours ever.

Reading his Lordship's sentiments over again, I am inclined to think that in all I have said, I have only given him back the same in other terms. He disallows both the absolute *free* and the absolute *close;* so do I, and, if I understand myself, have said so in my Preface. He wishes to recommend a medium, though he will not call it so; so do I, — only we express it differently. What is it, then, we dispute about? My head is not good enough to-day to discover.[1]

CXI.

STANZAS TO MRS. UNWIN.

To Mary.[2]

THE twentieth year is wellnigh past,
Since first our sky was overcast;
Ah, would that this might be the last!
      My Mary!

---

[1] Although Cowper's life was prolonged more than six years after this date, this is the last of his letters free from traces of a disordered mind. The combined influences of Mrs. Unwin's decline, her death in 1796, and his own morbid thoughts, gave to his correspondence a tone so abnormal, so steeped in the gloomy and unnatural fancies of the melancholia that terminated only with his death, that these later letters can be given no place in a collection designed to represent Cowper at his best.

[2] The exact date of the composition of these lines is not known; Hayley believed it to be the last original piece which Cowper produced while living at Weston, and questions "whether any language on earth can exhibit a specimen of verse more exquisitely tender."

Thy spirits have a fainter flow,
I see thee daily weaker grow;
'T was my distress that brought thee low,
    My Mary!

Thy needles, once a shining store,
For my sake restless heretofore,
Now rust disused, and shine no more,
    My Mary!

For though thou gladly wouldst fulfil
The same kind office for me still,
Thy sight now seconds not thy will,
    My Mary!

But well thou play'dst the housewife's part;
And all thy threads, with magic art,
Have wound themselves about this heart,
    My Mary!

Thy indistinct expressions seem
Like language utter'd in a dream;
Yet me they charm, whate'er the theme,
    My Mary!

Thy silver locks, once auburn bright,
Are still more lovely in my sight
Than golden beams of orient light,
    My Mary!

For could I view nor them nor thee,
What sight worth seeing could I see?
The sun would rise in vain for me,
    My Mary!

Partakers of thy sad decline,
Thy hands their little force resign;
Yet gently prest, press gently mine,
    My Mary!

Such feebleness of limbs thou prov'st,
That now at every step thou mov'st
Upheld by two; — yet still thou lov'st,
        My Mary!

And still to love, though prest with ill,
In wintry age to feel no chill,
With me is to be lovely still,
        My Mary!

But ah! by constant heed I know
How oft the sadness that I show
Transforms thy smiles to looks of woe,
        My Mary!

And should my future lot be cast
With much resemblance of the past,
Thy worn-out heart will break at last,
        My Mary!

THE END.